MASTER QUILTER'S WOR~~~~~

ILLUSTRATED
GUIDE TO
English Paper Piecing™

By Jodi Warner

HOUSE of
WHITE
BIRCHES
PUBLISHERS
SINCE 1947

Table of Contents

Projects

ILLUSTRATED GUIDE TO ENGLISH PAPER PIECING is published by House of White Birches, 306 East Parr Road, Berne, IN 46711, telephone (260) 589-4000. Printed in USA. Copyright © 2004 House of White Birches.

HOUSE of WHITE BIRCHES PUBLISHERS SINCE 1947

RETAILERS: If you would like to carry this pattern book or any other House of White Birches publications, call the Wholesale Department at Annie's Attic to set up a direct account: (903) 636-4303. Also, request a complete listing of publications available from House of White Birches.

E-mail: Customer_Service@whitebirches.com

Editors: Jeanne Stauffer, Sandra L. Hatch; **Associate Editor:** Dianne Schmidt; **Technical Artist:** Connie Rand; **Copy Editors:** Michelle Beck, Sue Harvey, Nicki Lehman; **Graphic Artist:** Ronda Bechinski; **Photography:** Kelly Heydinger, Christena Green; **Photography Stylist:** Tammy Nussbaum

Library of Congress Number: 2002109339
ISBN: 1-59217-009-9   1 2 3 4 5 6 7 8 9

Introduction to English Paper Piecing

English paper piecing is a hand-piecing technique that uses paper shapes as foundations to accurately prepare patchwork pieces for joining. Each trimmed paper shape is basted, pinned or attached with fabric glue stick to the wrong side of a larger fabric patch. Seam allowances are folded to the back at the paper edge and basted in place. The prepared, finished-size shapes are then joined using a whipstitch through fabric folded edges.

Almost any shape can be prepared using English paper piecing, but it is usually reserved for more complex shapes. These include trapezoids, diamonds and, most familiarly, the hexagon seen in the traditional Grandmother's Flower Garden settings. One reason this technique makes sense for these shapes is that they often require inset seaming at intersections. The whipstitch used for joining edges allows the progressing seam to pivot and continue at corners, thereby simplifying construction at joints.

Another advantage involves tactile appeal. Prepared shapes have a satisfying feel and manageability, in some ways akin to fitting puzzle pieces. Work in progress is also very portable, space conserving, comfortably repetitive and straightforward.

The bouquet of quilts presented here range from easy-to-execute to more complex and time intensive. Where one design may use miniaturized hexagons, another is stitched with oversize diamonds. Some projects use only one shape, others combine several, and two employ English paper-pieced panels as the foundation for appliqué details. Techniques and tips demonstrate the various foundation materials that can be used, including photocopies attached with a glue stick, mass-cut freezer paper for iron fusings and reusable plastic and Mylar shapes.

Hand piecing is used in the majority of projects, but some have machine-stitched seams within the foundation shapes. Two are even more innovative, joining prepared shapes with invisible machine stitching. Within this wide variety, there will be something to intrigue any quilter, whether trying this technique for the first time, or seeking refinement and challenge for skills already mastered.

MEET THE DESIGNER

Jodi Glissmeyer Warner finds inspiration for most of her captivating designs between 5 and 7:30 a.m. while her husband, Vince, and their three children, ranging in ages from 12 to 18 years, are still sleeping. Her studio is in her home in the rural/residential area of South Jordan, Utah, and she finds it a wonderful way to work. As the day progresses, she can enjoy executing her designs in fabric while interacting almost constantly with her family.

Jodi was raised in the Holladay community, southeast of Salt Lake City. She learned to sew at a very young age. She received a B.A. degree in textiles/fashion design from Brigham Young University in 1978, and began designing and making costumes for a theatrical studio and gowns for a bridal shop.

As a new homemaker Jodi found she enjoyed applying traditional patchwork and appliqué methods to the decorating needs of her home. She soon realized she had found a design arena that offered endless challenges and rewards.

Jodi has lectured, conducted workshops, taught at Salt Lake area quilt shops and mounted one-woman quilt shows in the inter-mountain West. She was an instructor for three years for a lifelong-learning curriculum through the University of Utah.

Jodi's quilts have won local, regional and national awards, most notably her *Twelfth Night Tally*, which won third place/professional appliqué at the 1993 competition of the American Quilter's Society. Her patterns and articles about her work have appeared in many magazines. She also owns her own pattern business, Hearthsewn, a natural outgrowth of the requests from students and area shops for formalized patterns of the designs she teaches. The company was established in 1986 and includes more than three dozen patterns, an annual Christmas stocking and patchwork clothing.

A current interest of Jodi's centers around a growing collection of quilts paired with children's storybooks, which she uses to promote family literacy and quiltmaking awareness.

English Paper Piecing for Hexagons

English paper piecing is a technique that uses paper shapes as the foundations to accurately prepare the patchwork pieces.

NOTES

The trimmed paper shape is basted, pinned or glued to the backside center of a fabric patch that has seam allowances added. The seam allowances are folded over the paper edge and basted into the finished size. The prepared shapes are then joined using a whipstitch along the folded edges of the fabrics.

While many shapes may be used with this technique, including triangles, trapezoids, squares and diamonds,

the most familiar shape is the hexagon seen in traditional Grandmother's Flower Garden settings.

Prepared shapes have a satisfying feel and manipulative appeal, in some ways akin to school puzzle pieces. This may account for some of the appeal. Work in progress is also very portable, space conserving, comfortably repetitive and simple. Inaccuracies sometimes encountered with other techniques can be corrected because of the immediate visual feedback as the pieces fit together.

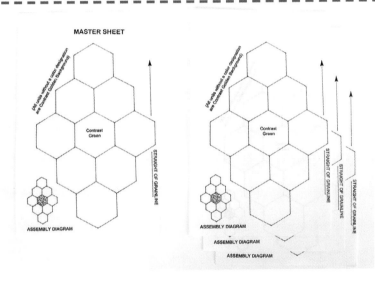

1

PREPARING & CUTTING PIECES

1A. Obtain or prepare a layout master that includes finished-size hexagons for a construction unit of a specific project. Trimming is easier if the shapes share adjacent sides as much as possible. Make photocopies on regular-weight white paper.

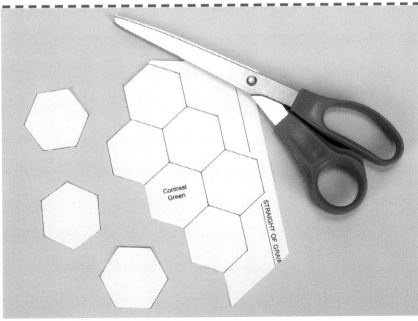

1B. Carefully cut out each hexagon shape. Where shapes share a drawn line, split the line with scissor blades.

1C. Prepare a patch cutting template by adding seam allowance (¼" or very slightly larger) to one finished-size paper hexagon. Trace and cut out hexagon fabric patches from the appropriate fabrics in required quantities.

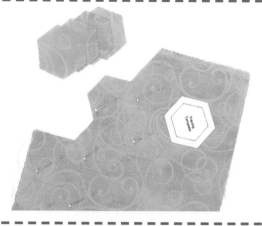

1D. Center and secure one paper shape against the wrong side of the fabric patch. Follow any grain-line recommendations included on the master sheet.

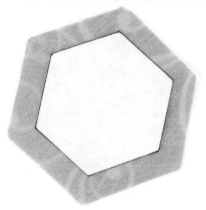

2

SEWING

2A. Single-thread a fine hand-sewing needle with light-colored basting thread; knot the end (dark color thread used in photo sample). Fold and finger-press or pinch the first fabric edge back precisely at the paper-shape edge. Baste through fabric and paper layers, stopping near opposite edge and corner of enclosed paper shape.

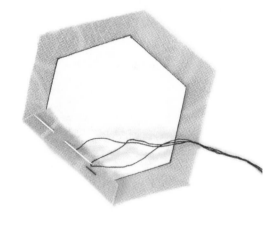

2B. Fold and finger-press the second edge back at the paper edges as before, this time including the folded-over seam allowance from the first side. Aim for crisp and precise edges and corners. See photo 3B on page 8 to see the wrong side with all edges folded over.

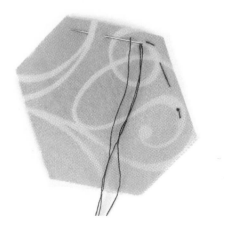

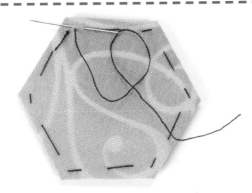

2C. Continue to fold and finger-press each succeeding edge as before for all remaining edges. Secure basting end with a small backstitch with needle piercing only the top fabric layer, easily visible from front for removal later. Trim thread, leaving a ¼" tail.

2D. Prepare all the hexagon shapes required for specified construction unit. Position in layout order for reference during joining.

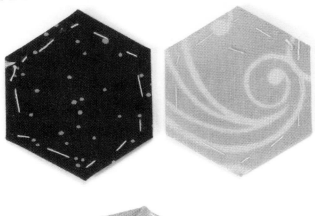

JOINING PATCHES

3A. Begin with center and one adjacent hexagon. Identify the edges to be joined, then layer them right sides together. If edges appear slightly different in length, match corner points and ease in the difference when whipstitching. Once the paper is removed, any bowing this may cause will relax and fabric will flatten.

Tip

Since the hexagons are symmetrical shapes and many sides will align when layered together, take care to focus on the edges to be joined. Positioning the shapes in layout order and visualizing how they fit from the front side of the work before each new shape is added will assure accuracy.

3B. Single-thread a fine hand-sewing needle with matching thread. Secure end with an overhand knot. At top corner, insert needle under seam allowance and out corner tip of top patch.

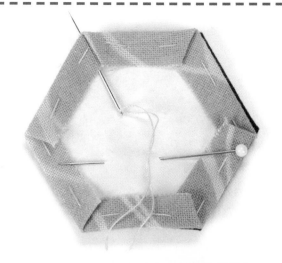

3C. Insert needle through lower layer and upper layer fabric folds exactly at the corner. Needle should catch only 1 or 2 threads at the folded edge of the patch and miss or only barely pierce enclosed paper edge. Thread between stitches will wrap around fabric folded edges in a whipstitch. Secure this corner—and each corner throughout construction—by taking a second stitch exactly through the corner.

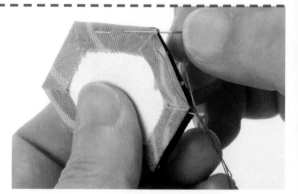

Tip

Stitches need not be so close as to resemble buttonhole or satin stitching, but close enough to secure the patches. Put moderate tension on each stitch as thread is drawn up. A thimble is recommended for precise, painless stitching.

3D. Using fairly close stitches (12–14 per inch), continue whipstitching along the edges to be joined.

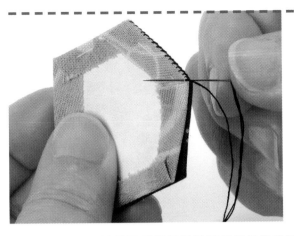

3E. At the opposite corner, secure with two stitches exactly through corner. (Contrast thread is used here to show the stitch-length gauge.)

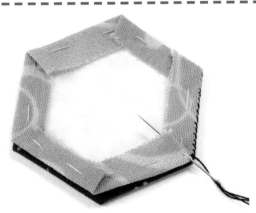

3F. To tie off or end a sequence (or when thread in needle has been used up), slip needle through the final stitch loop before it is pulled tight to anchor. Insert needle under top layer of seam allowance, to exit toward the patch's center. Pull thread up and cut the tail even with the seam allowance edge. As stitching reaches a corner and another patch can be added at the edges adjacent to the corner where the thread is attached, do not anchor and skip to 3H.

3G. Open patches flat.

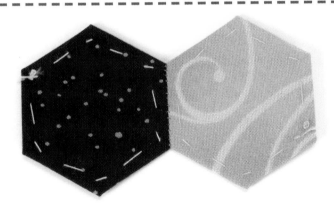

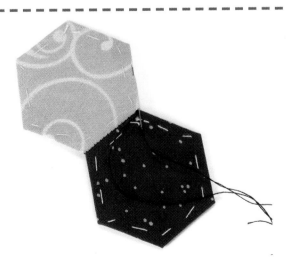

3H. Follow this procedure for continuous stitching of center and ring sequence common to Grandmother's Flower Garden and other layouts. Insert needle between fabric layers within fold tunnel, then slide toward and out at opposite corner. When hexagon edges are longer than a needle length, exit the needle through edge at the halfway point.

Tip

To assist edge to open flat, unfold front sides outward and continue until paper sides are touching. Finger-crease edge; then unfold to flat position.

Tip

When joining the six hexagons around a center, always work from the outer edge back toward the center so that the needle will end at the best corner for continuing on.

3I. Position and identify the first edges to be joined; layer the next hexagon patch right sides together. Pass the needle through both patches at the center point, then repeat a stitch in place to tack the edges.

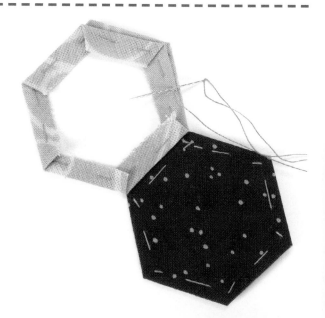

Tip

Whipstitch up to the tack stitch, skip over and continue closely on the other side.

Tip

Fold the center hexagon in half along the extended line of the pivot center. It will be necessary to fold the work whenever the edge connection process requires the pivot. Don't let the stiffness of the paper interfere with manipulation necessary to stitch accurately.

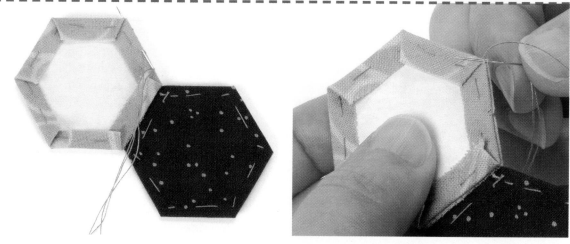

3J. Pass the needle through the tunnel in the fold to the top corner. Complete corner stitches; then stitch down along the edges to the opposite corner and repeat the anchor stitches.

3K. Pivot the second edge of the upper patch to align to its appropriate mate. Secure corner, whipstitch across edge and secure at opposite corner.

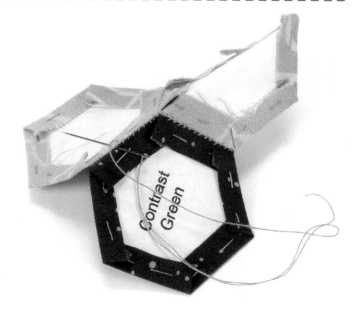

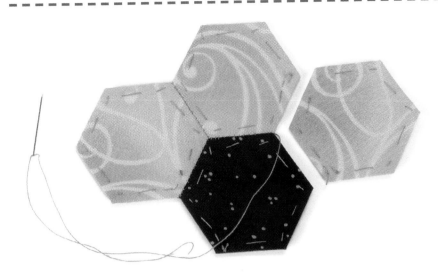

3L. Open the seam as described in 3G, then position and repeat the joining process for each subsequent hexagon to complete the ring around the center.

3M. When the unit is complete, press lightly with a moderately warm iron. See completed unit in photo 2E on page 14.

4

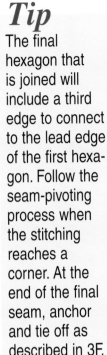

> *Tip*
> The final hexagon that is joined will include a third edge to connect to the lead edge of the first hexagon. Follow the seam-pivoting process when the stitching reaches a corner. At the end of the final seam, anchor and tie off as described in 3F.

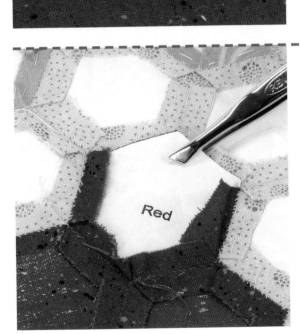

COMBINING UNITS

4A. Combine units to complete the panel or section; press. To remove basting, work from the front side to first snip off basting knots, then slip final anchoring stitch free; finally, pull basting from each patch.

4B. Turn patchwork to the backside, slip fingers or tweezers under overlapping seam allowance to lift paper edge; remove each paper shape.

Red

> *Tip*
> Leave paper shapes basted in place until completion of all joined seams. If edge finish will follow the hexagon edge, make sure the edge creases remain visible. If the edge finish will be straight-trimmed with borders added, leave paper shapes in place as stabilizer until trimming is complete.

Refer to the following step-by-step photos to help you with the construction processes for Poinsettia Paradise.

1

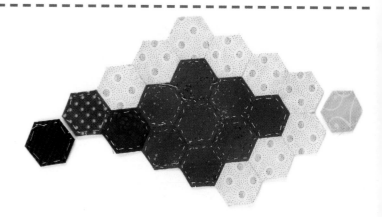

MAKING BLOSSOMS

1A . Prepare and join hexagons for A petal sections. Also prepare one green plaid hexagon for blossom center. An additional tan scroll hexagon will be required when joining blossoms into rows.

1B. Blossoms are composed of six A petal sections. Position A petal sections side by side to visualize which edges will be joined.

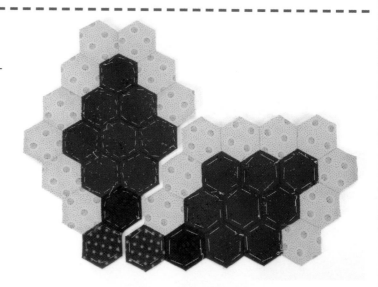

1C. Focus on the first edge to be joined along aligned edges. Carefully lay one A section over so that first edges of target hexagon to be joined remain lined up. Pin and begin stitching. When stitching of one hexagon edge is complete, leave thread attached and pivot petal edges to align

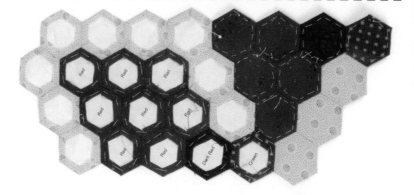

the next pair of edges. Continue stitching until all adjacent edges of petals are joined. Tie off one thread color and attach matching thread as needed.

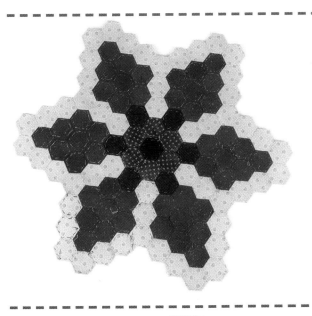

1D. As the first two petal sections are joined, align and attach green plaid hexagon at blossom center. Continue joining until blossom is complete.

MAKING HALF BLOSSOMS

2A. Half blossoms are composed of two A petal sections with one B section and one C half-petal section.

2B. Samples of sections here show temporary side-edge seam line traced through extending hexagons. Excess will eventually be trimmed away ¼" beyond traced line.

2C. Arrange two A sections with B and C to visualize edges to join. Then join into complete half-blossom unit.

2D. Joined half-blossom unit.

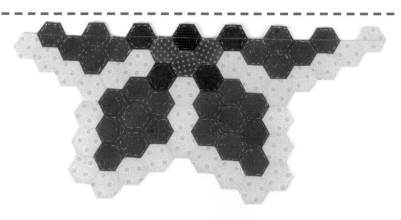

2E. Spaces between large blossom shapes are filled in with diamond-shape D sections.

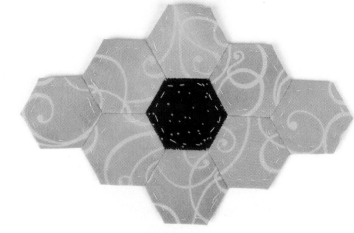

2F. Section E half-diamond shapes will complete the center panel side edges. Arrange and join hexagons to form these sections as shown.

3

ROW ASSEMBLY

3A. Begin row assembly by joining three full blossoms; connect with two D diamonds between and E half diamonds at each end. Also join additional D diamond sections in angles between blossom petal extensions as shown.

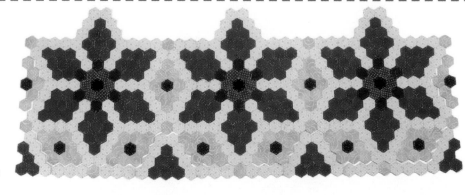

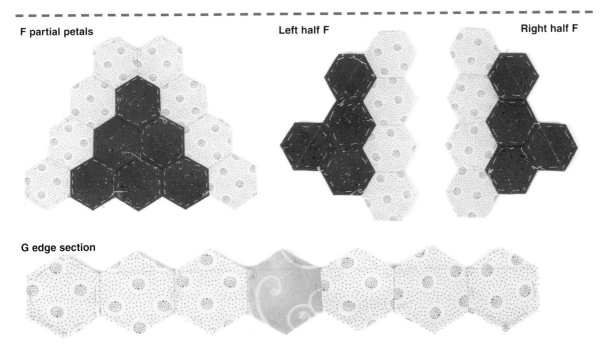

F partial petals **Left half F** **Right half F**

G edge section

3B. To square up top edge, prepare two F partial petals, one right half F, one left half F and three G edge sections as shown.

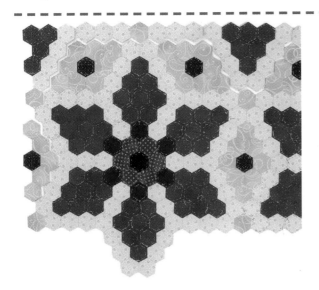

3C. Arrange and join edge sections to complete straight panel edge as shown.

3D. Assemble the next row by joining full and half blossoms with D diamond sections between blossoms and in angles at row upper edge; add joiner hexagons in opening at diamond tips.

D diamond sections

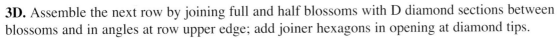
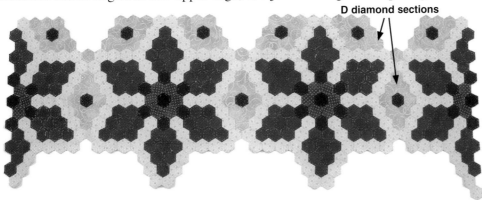

3E. Position and join row by fitting petal extensions of top row between D diamonds and inserting joiner hexagons into the openings at petal and diamond tips.

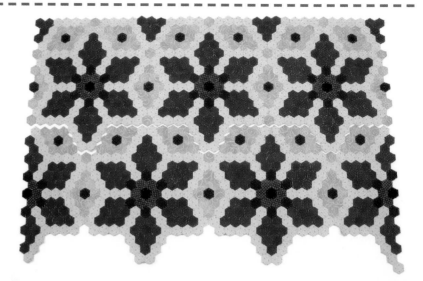

3F. Continue assembling alternate rows and joining to center panel. When fourth row is in place, arrange and join F, G and H edge sections to create straight panel bottom edge.

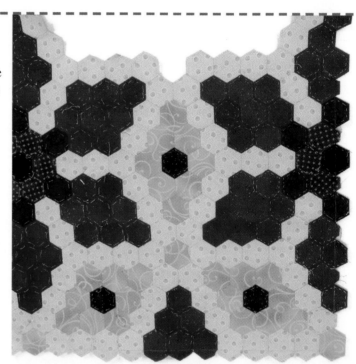

TRIMMING EDGES SQUARE

4A. Center panel edges must be trimmed square before borders are added. For top and bottom edges, use a straightedge to trace a temporary guideline as shown as trim guidelines on sections B, C and E. For side edges, trace a temporary guideline as shown as trim guidelines on sections F, G and H. Release basting along receding hexagon edges and unfold seam allowances flat. Position rotary ruler ¼" beyond traced line and trim.

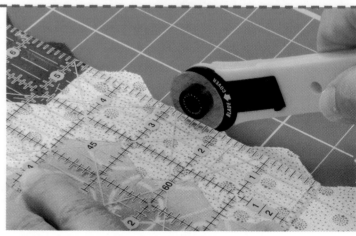

4B. Since paper foundations are still in place, trimming steps will cut away both excess paper and fabric at edge.

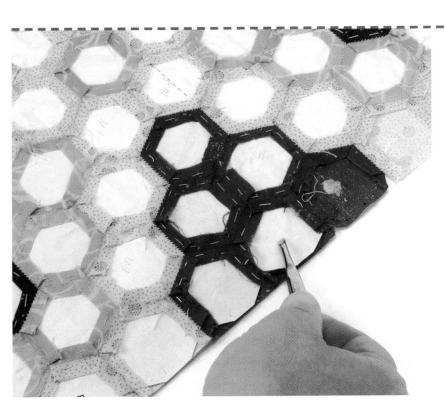

4C. Remove basting and paper foundations.

Poinsettia Paradise

*Nearly 1,900 hexagons are used to construct this original poinsettia variation,
a distant cousin of the traditional Grandmother's Flower Garden.*

PROJECT SPECIFICATIONS
Skill Level: Intermediate
Quilt Size: Approximately 69" x 84"

MATERIALS
- ¼ yard green speckled
- ¼ yard green plaid
- ⅓ yard dark red mottled
- 1 yard green-with-tan dots
- 1¼ yards tan scroll
- 3 yards red tone-on-tone
- 4 yards cream tone-on-tone
- Thin cotton batting 75" x 90"
- Backing 75" x 90"
- Neutral color all-purpose thread
- Contrasting quilting thread
- 9 yards ⅛" poly cord for optional dual binding
- Basic sewing tools and supplies and water-erasable marker or pencil

INSTRUCTIONS

CONSTRUCTING UNITS

Step 1. Before beginning, photocopy patterns in quantities noted on diagrams. ***Note:*** *Ignore quilting lines within sections; these will be transferred to the quilt top using conventional methods at the appropriate time.*

Step 2. Refer to step-by-step illustrations for English Paper Piecing for Hexagons on page 5 to complete one A petal section as shown in Figure 1; repeat for 68 A petal sections. Prepare 14 green plaid hexagons for blossom centers using the joiner hexagon template.

Figure 1
Complete an A petal section.

Step 3. Complete 10 full blossoms. For each full blossom, arrange six A petal sections in a circle around a green plaid center hexagon, with green-with-tan dots hexagons aligned to form a center ring as shown in Figure 2. Join edges as arranged; press the completed full blossom. Repeat to make 10 full blossoms.

Step 4. Complete four B and C sections using photocopied patterns. Arrange and join one each B and C section with two A sections and one green plaid center for a half blossom as shown in Figure 3. Join edges as arranged; press. Repeat to make four half-blossom units. ***Note:*** *To produce the straight side edges along which the half blossoms fall, whole hexagons will later be trimmed ¼ beyond dashed lines shown in section diagrams. We are working only with whole hexagons.*

Figure 2
Arrange 6 A sections in a circle around the center hexagon, with green-with-tan dots hexagons aligned to form a ring for 1 blossom unit.

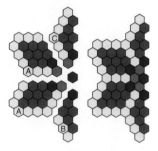

Figure 3
Arrange and join 1 each B and C section with 2 A sections and 1 green plaid center for a half blossom.

Step 5. Complete 40 D diamonds, four E half diamonds, five F sections, one left and one right half-F section, five G sections and two H sections as shown in Figure 4, working only with whole hexagons.

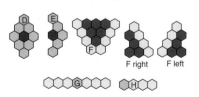

F right   F left

Figure 4
Complete sections as shown.

QUILT TOP ASSEMBLY

Step 1. Arrange three full blossoms, two D diamonds and two E half diamonds for row 1 as shown in Figure 5; join units. Repeat for row 3.

Figure 5
Complete rows 1 and 3 as shown.

Step 2. Arrange two full blossoms, two half blossoms and three D diamonds for row 2 as shown in Figure 6; join units. Repeat for row 4.

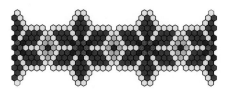

Figure 6
Complete rows 2 and 4 as shown.

Step 3. Join alternating rows, offsetting blossom points and inserting D diamonds between adjacent blossoms as shown in Figure 7.

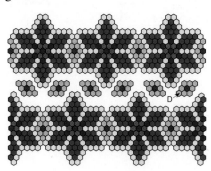

Figure 7
Join rows, offsetting blossom points and inserting D diamonds between adjacent blossoms.

Step 4. Prepare and join single tan scroll blossom hexagons in the openings between blossom tips as shown in Figure 8.

Figure 8
Insert tan scroll hexagons into openings between rows.

Step 5. For panel top and bottom edges, add D diamonds on each side of blossom points and insert F and half-F

sections in place of blossom or half-blossom units referring to Figure 9.

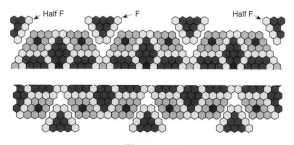

Figure 9
Arrange F and half-F sections along top and bottom panel edges.

Step 6. Position and join sections G and H in upper and lower edge rows between F sections referring to Figure 10. Position tan scroll hexagons in openings at F-section tips as shown in Figure 11.

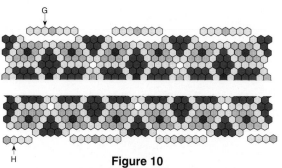

Figure 10
Arrange G and H sections in upper and lower edge rows between F sections.

Figure 11
Position tan scroll hexagons in openings at F-section tips.

Figure 12
Position the 1/4" guideline along the trim line of B, C, E, half-F and H sections and trim to make straight side edges.

Step 7. To trim panel side edges, position the 1/4" rotary-ruler guideline along the trim line of B, C, E, half-F and H sections and trim as shown in Figure 12.

Step 8. To trim upper and lower panel edges, repeat Step 7 using trim line on F, half-F, G and H sections.

Step 9. Remove all basting and paper shapes.

ADDING BORDERS

Step 1. Cut and piece two 2" x 69½" I and two 2" x 57½" J strips cream tone-on-tone. Sew I to opposite long sides and J to the top and bottom of the center panel; press seams toward I and J strips.

Step 2. Cut and piece two 1¾" x 72½" K and two 1¾" x 60" L strips red tone-on-tone. Sew K to opposite long sides and L to the top and bottom of the center panel; press seams toward K and L strips.

Step 3. Cut and piece two 5¼" x 75" M and two 5¼" x 69½" N strips cream tone-on-tone. Sew M to opposite long sides and N to the top and bottom of the center panel; press seams toward M and N strips.

FINISHING THE QUILT

Step 1. Transfer quilting designs to petals, center ring and diamonds. Mark border pattern of choice. Also mark ¼" echo quilting lines inside each green plaid hexagon, beyond dark edges of blossom units and beyond tan scroll hexagons.

Step 2. Sandwich thin cotton batting between the completed quilt top and prepared backing piece; pin or baste layers together to hold.

Step 3. Quilt on marked lines; when quilting is complete, remove pins or basting.

Step 4. Prepare 320" of ⅞"-wide bias from green-with-tan dots. Fold around the ⅛" poly cord and stitch close to cord to make piping. Baste piping around quilt edges.

Step 5. Prepare 320" of 2¼"-wide bias binding from red tone-on-tone and apply to edges on top of piping to finish. *Note: The piping will be seen between the border edge and the binding edge as shown in the close-up photo below.* ❖

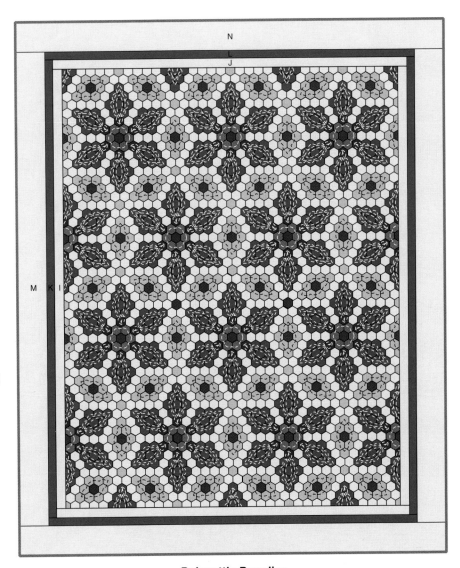

Poinsettia Paradise
Placement Diagram
Approximately 69" x 84"

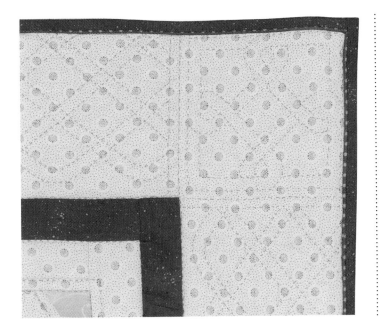

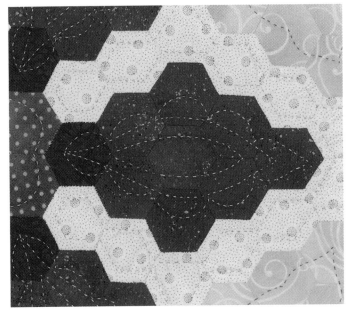

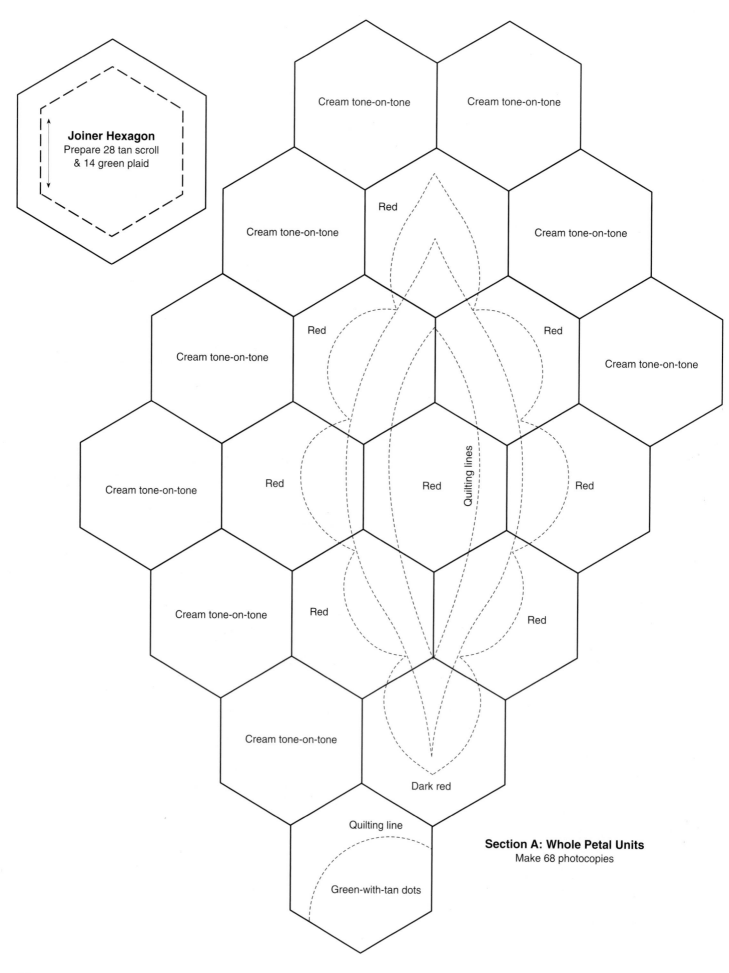

Joiner Hexagon
Prepare 28 tan scroll
& 14 green plaid

Cream tone-on-tone

Cream tone-on-tone

Red

Cream tone-on-tone

Cream tone-on-tone

Red

Red

Cream tone-on-tone

Red

Cream tone-on-tone

Cream tone-on-tone

Red

Red

Red

Quilting lines

Cream tone-on-tone

Red

Red

Cream tone-on-tone

Dark red

Quilting line

Section A: Whole Petal Units
Make 68 photocopies

Green-with-tan dots

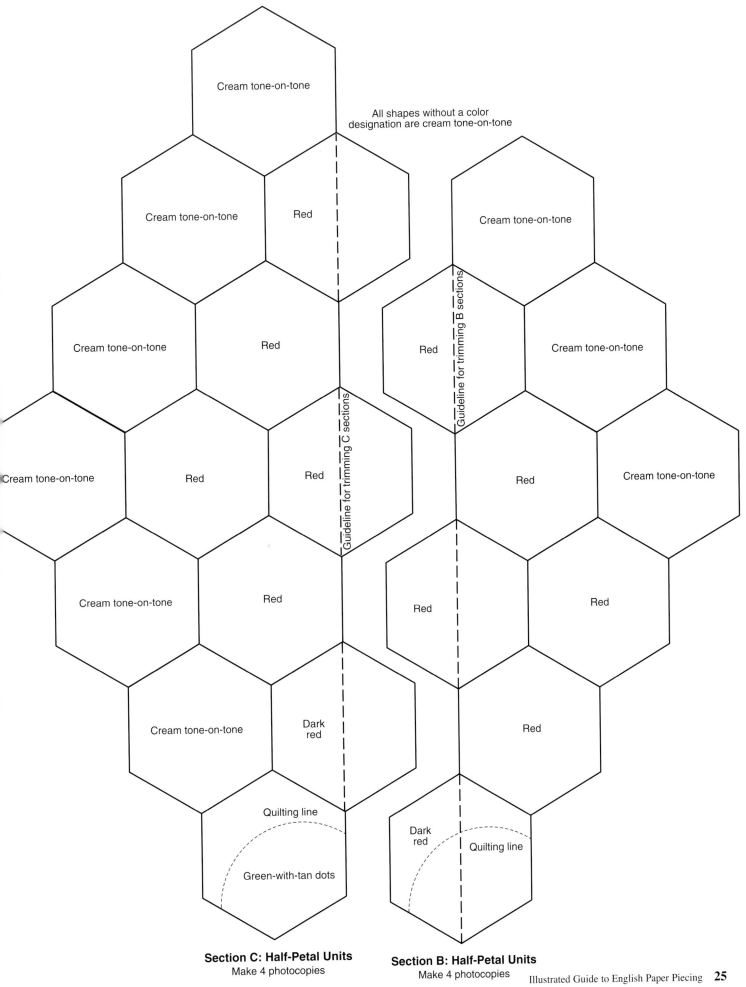

Cream tone-on-tone

All shapes without a color
designation are cream tone-on-tone

Cream tone-on-tone

Red

Cream tone-on-tone

Cream tone-on-tone

Red

Red

Cream tone-on-tone

Guideline for trimming B sections

Cream tone-on-tone

Red

Red

Cream tone-on-tone

Guideline for trimming C sections

Red

Red

Red

Cream tone-on-tone

Cream tone-on-tone

Red

Red

Red

Red

Cream tone-on-tone

Dark
red

Red

Quilting line

Dark
red

Quilting line

Green-with-tan dots

Section C: Half-Petal Units
Make 4 photocopies

Section B: Half-Petal Units
Make 4 photocopies

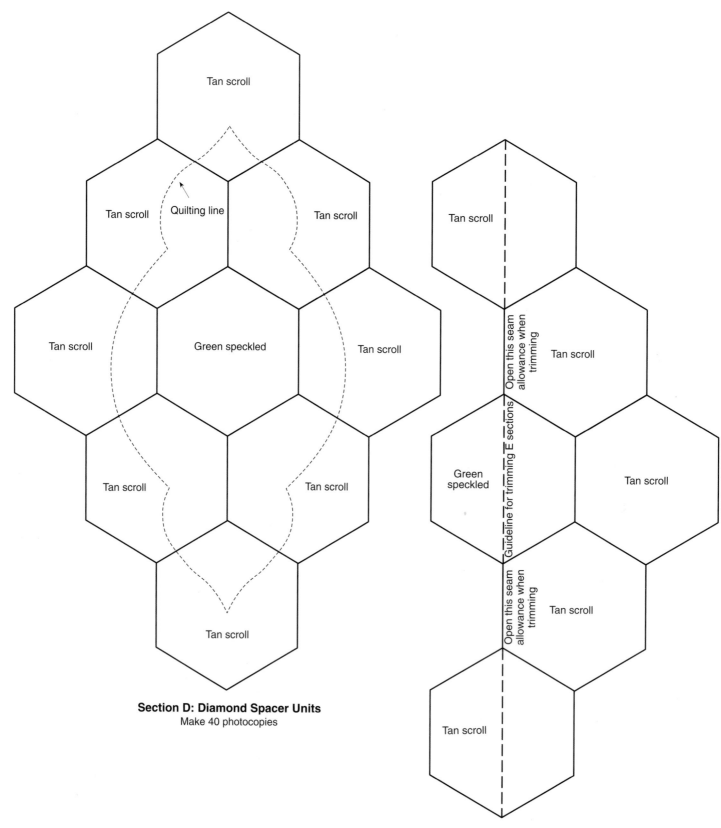

Section D: Diamond Spacer Units
Make 40 photocopies

Tan scroll

Tan scroll   Quilting line   Tan scroll

Tan scroll   Green speckled   Tan scroll

Tan scroll   Tan scroll

Tan scroll

Section E: Half-Diamond Spacer Units
Make 4 photocopies

Tan scroll

Tan scroll

Green speckled   Tan scroll

Tan scroll

Tan scroll

Open this seam allowance when trimming

Guideline for trimming E sections

Open this seam allowance when trimming

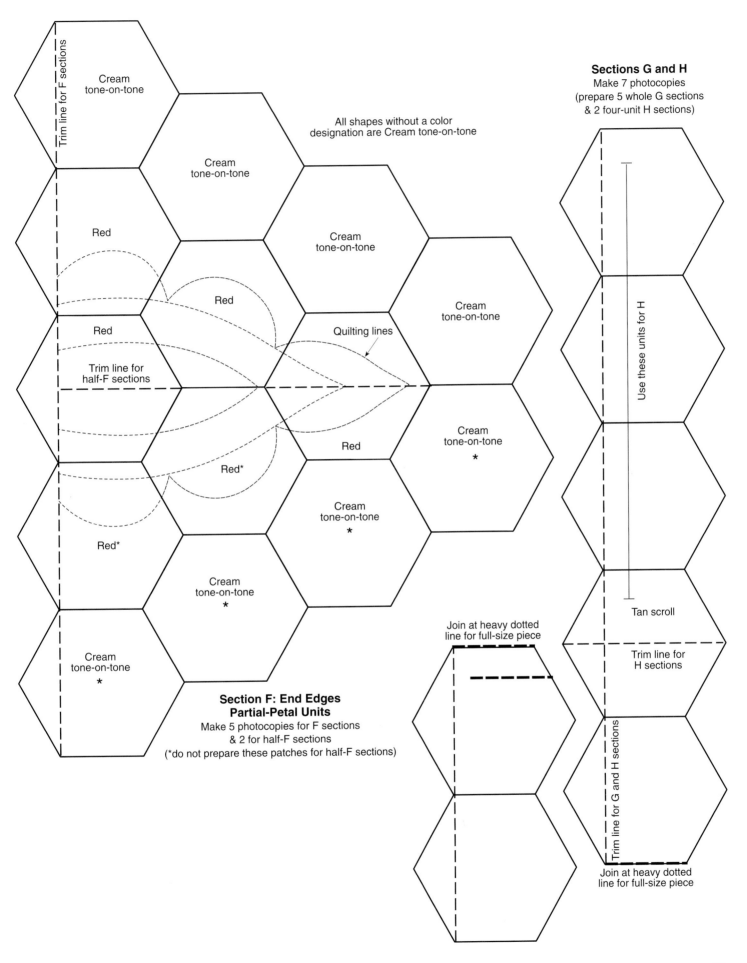

Trim line for F sections

Cream
tone-on-tone

Cream
tone-on-tone

All shapes without a color
designation are Cream tone-on-tone

Cream
tone-on-tone

Red

Red

Cream
tone-on-tone

Red

Red

Cream
tone-on-tone

Quilting lines

Trim line for
half-F sections

Red

Cream
tone-on-tone
*

Red*

Cream
tone-on-tone
*

Red*

Cream
tone-on-tone
*

**Section F: End Edges
Partial-Petal Units**
Make 5 photocopies for F sections
& 2 for half-F sections
(*do not prepare these patches for half-F sections)

Cream
tone-on-tone
*

Sections G and H
Make 7 photocopies
(prepare 5 whole G sections
& 2 four-unit H sections)

Use these units for H

Tan scroll

Trim line for
H sections

Trim line for G and H sections

Join at heavy dotted
line for full-size piece

Join at heavy dotted
line for full-size piece

Edge Finishing for Hexagon Foundation Quilts

Quilts with hexagon edges are difficult to bind using traditional methods. Try butting the edges and hand-stitching backing and top edges together at the edge to finish referring to these step-by-step instructions.

1

JOINING THE UNITS

1A . Speed the foundation-cutting process and assist construction by preparing a four-layer section of freezer paper. Position hexagon diagrams on top of layers and staple through each shape to secure. Cut out precisely through all layers. To use, remove staples and iron-fuse plastic side to the wrong side of fabric patches.

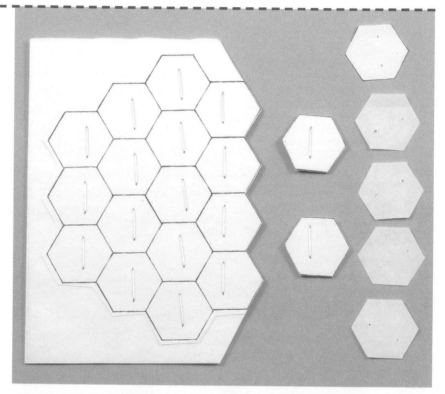

1B. Prepare foundation-pieced hexagon patches for each blossom unit. Join petal hexagons to the center hexagon; then join five background hexagons to edges as shown. Assemble three joined units side by side into first row, then continue adding units.

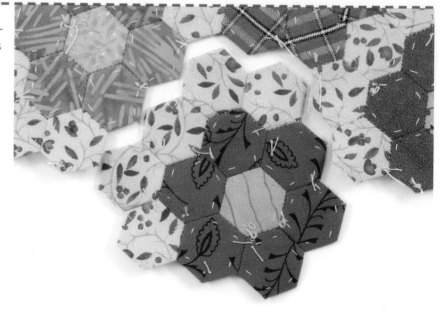

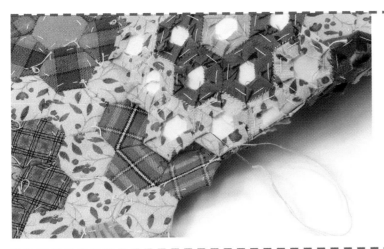

1C. When attaching units to panel assembly, align flat to visualize the edge that will join. Carefully lay single unit over assembly with first edges aligned and right sides together; stitch edge, pivoting after each edge is completed to align the next edges and stitch.

1D. When all blossom units have been joined, some vacant positions will remain at the edges. Attach individual background shapes to form a complete row of background at outer edges.

2

FINISHING EDGES

2A. Layer the pieced top with batting and backing and quilt, leaving areas next to edge unquilted. Trim excess batting and backing 1/4" beyond folded edge of outer row.

Tip
Leave paper foundations of outer row ONLY in place through the quilting process until this step is complete to preserve the basted finished edge shape of quilt top.

2B. Fold top edge out of the way and trim excess batting 1/16" smaller than quilt top, so that the batting edge is just short of the folded edge when stitching is complete. Trimming this way keeps batting out of the way of folded edges that will be joined.

2C. Transfer the folded edge of top to the wrong side of the attached backing using a straightedge.

Tip

When finishing the complex edge with larger-scale hexagons, stay stitching is only needed ¼" on each side of corners.

2D. Fold the stepped shape of the backing under for a clean edge finish, clipping to the inside corners through backing seam allowance ONLY. To protect the edge against fraying and pulling apart, complete a hand stay stitch along the marked line with matching thread.

clipped corners

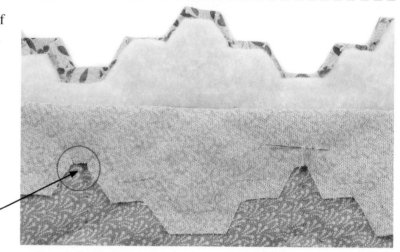

Tip

Once the edge shape has been transferred to inside of backing edge, paper foundation shapes can be removed at any time. However, leaving them in place until just prior to completing the edge stitching will better preserve the folded edges until needed.

2E. Fold the backing seam allowance under exactly on stay-stitched and traced lines.

2F. Invisibly-stitch folded edges of top and backing by hand using a ladder stitch that moves back and forth between the folded edges. When the edge is fully stitched, complete remaining quilting near edges.

Season's Splendor

Nineteen small blossoms made up of hexagons evoke a flurry of petals for a festive tabletop. Change colors to reflect different seasonal themes.

PROJECT SPECIFICATIONS

Skill Level: Beginner

Quilt Size: Approximately 16" x 14⅞"

MATERIALS

- Scraps 19 different rust and yellow prints
- ⅓ yard tan print for background
- Thin cotton batting 19" x 18"
- Backing 19" x 18"
- Neutral color all-purpose thread
- Contrasting quilting thread
- Fabric glue stick
- Paper for foundation piecing
- Basic sewing tools and supplies and water-erasable marker or pencil

INSTRUCTIONS

Cutting

Step 1. Prepare a template for A using the pattern given; cut as directed on the piece.

Step 2. Pair rust petals and yellow centers together in pleasing combinations. Tack paired fabrics together with quick basting stitches for easy handling.

Step 3. Make and cut apart 14 photocopies of the hexagon master for English paper piecing.

Step 4. To construct each blossom unit, center and glue-stick paper shapes against the wrong side of six petal, one center and five background hexagons.

Step 5. Fold seam allowance over paper edges and baste all around each shape as shown in Figure 1.

Figure 1
Fold seam allowance over paper edges
and baste all around each shape.

PIECING BLOSSOM UNITS

Step 1. Sew six petals to one center as shown in Figure 2 to complete one blossom. *Note: Refer to English Paper Piecing for Hexagons on page 5 for stitching method.*

Figure 2
Join petals to center to
complete 1 blossom.

Figure 3
Sew 5 background
shapes to blossom
edges to complete
1 blossom unit.

Step 2. Sew five background shapes to blossom edges as shown in Figure 3 to complete one blossom unit; repeat for 19 blossom units.

TOP ASSEMBLY

Step 1. Position three blossom units side by side for top row, inserting background hexagons into angles of adjacent blossom shapes as shown in Figure 4; join units.

Figure 4
Arrange blossom units as shown for top row.

Step 2. For second row, position four units side by side along lower edge of row 1 as shown in Figure 5. Rotate units as needed to fit into row 1 openings. *Note: Extra background hexagons will be added to fill in open areas along outer edge later.* Join units as arranged.

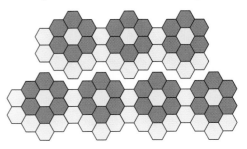

Figure 5
Position 4 units side by side
along lower edge of row 1.

Step 3. For row 3, position five units side by side below row 2 and join referring to Figure 6. Repeat for rows 4 and 5 as for rows 2 and 1, again referring to Figure 6.

Step 4. Sew remaining background hexagons into the vacant spaces around the pieced unit to complete one row of background hexagons all around outside edge; press.

Step 5. Remove basting stitches and paper foundations from all hexagons except on the outer edge.

FINISHING THE QUILT
Step 1. Mark ¼" echo lines on rust hexagons around each

blossom center and lines through the center of each background hexagon using water-erasable marker or pencil.

Step 2. Sandwich thin cotton batting between the completed quilt top and prepared backing piece; pin or baste layers together to hold.

Step 3. Quilt on marked lines, leaving quilting lines next to outer edge unstitched until quilt edge is complete.

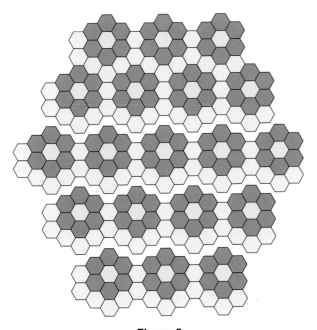

Figure 6
Position remaining rows and join as shown.

When quilting is complete, remove pins or basting.

Step 4. Trim excess backing ¼" beyond pieced top outer folded edges. *Note: Refer to page 26 Edge Finishing for Hexagon Foundation Quilts for step-by-step photo illustrations of the finishing process.*

Step 5. Trim excess batting ¹/₁₆" shorter than pieced top edge so that batting does not show beyond top edge.

Step 6. Use a short straightedge and sharp pencil to transfer top edge position to wrong side of backing.

Step 7. Stay-stitch through backing by hand with matching thread along marked line around entire mat perimeter.

Step 8. Carefully clip backing seam allowance at inside angles, stopping just short of stay stitching and traced line.

Step 9. Remove remaining basting and paper

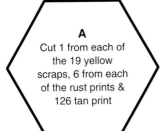

A
Cut 1 from each of the 19 yellow scraps, 6 from each of the rust prints & 126 tan print

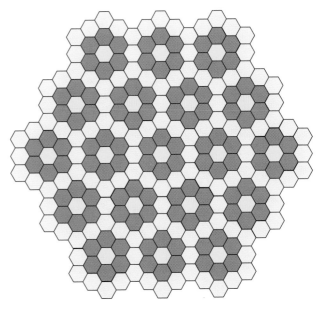

Season's Splendor
Placement Diagram
Approximately 16" x 14⅞"

founda-tions. Fold backing allowance along stay stitching, and baste in place.

Step 10. Join layers along folds with invisible stitches.

Step 11. Complete remaining quilting on marked lines near mat edges; remove basting. ❖

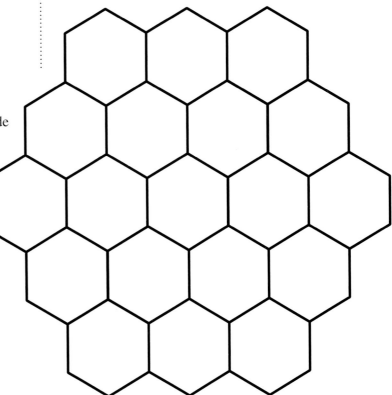

Hexagon Master
Make 14 photocopies

English Paper-Foundation Star Flower Shapes

Using the English paper-foundation method on a variety of angled shapes is easy to accomplish.

1

PREPARING FOR STITCHING

1A. The jewel-shaped foundation patch preparation incorporates hexagonlike corner angles and a diamond-like tip. The 120-degree hex corners will allow neat miterlike folding of seam allowances when folded back, but the 60-degree diamond points will require the seam allowance tail to extend beyond the shape's folded edge. Also pictured is a layered freezer-paper section for mass cutting of foundation shapes.

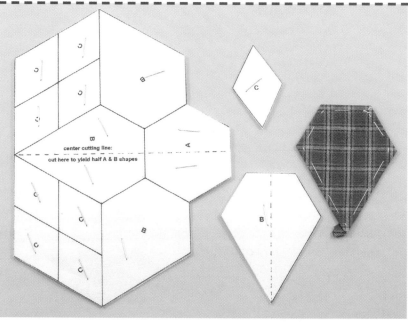

1B. Join six B jewel petals to A center hexagon to create whole blossom units.

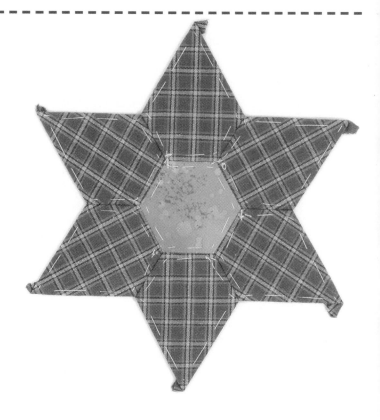

MAKING JEWEL UNITS

2A. Join one half B, one half BR and one half A with two whole B jewel petals to create half-blossom units that will square up the center panel at side edges.

2B. Prepare whole diamond units by joining rust and background C diamond patches.

Tip

Both pairs that complete the larger diamond unit can be joined in identical fashion. Rotate one joined pair to the final position with rust diamonds across the center and background at tips.

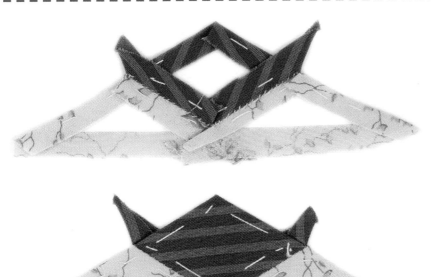

MAKING HALF-FILLER DIAMONDS

3A. Prepare half-filler diamonds by joining a single rust C and two background half-C diamond patches. Note that edges that will fall along panel edges are left unbasted. Prior to joining patchwork panel to border, excess seam allowance will be trimmed $1/4$" beyond paper edges of in-line patches.

3B. To square up top and bottom panel edges, prepare half-filler diamonds and join to D background half diamonds. Angled edges of D only and all edges of half C are folded and basted.  The assembled C section is then whipstitched to the prepared D foundation. The long edge of D remains unbasted. The tips are trimmed and the pieces joined later in border seams.

3C. The pieced border diamonds panel is prepared using diagonal sections of rust C diamonds and half-C background pieces. Long half-C edges remain unbasted. Border  panel edges will be trimmed and joined to borders.

3D. Join diagonal sections with end units to create the border panel. Trim excess seam allowance $1/4$" beyond the paper-foundation edges at each long panel edge.

Star Flowers

Jewel-shaped petals radiate from center hexagons in a compact field of posies.

PROJECT SPECIFICATIONS
Skill Level: Intermediate
Quilt Size: Approximately 54" x 66³/₄"

MATERIALS
- ¹/₄ yard rust mottled
- ¹/₄ yard goldenrod mottled
- ³/₄ yard rust stripe
- 1¹/₂ yards tan floral for background
- 2 yards teal stripe
- 2 yards teal/blue plaid
- Thin cotton batting 60" x 73"
- Backing 60" x 73"
- Neutral color all-purpose thread
- Contrasting quilting thread
- Stapler and staple remover
- Fabric glue stick
- 5 yards plastic-coated 18"-wide freezer paper
- Basic sewing tools and supplies and water-erasable marker or pencil

INSTRUCTIONS
Cutting

Step 1. Prepare templates using the pattern pieces given; cut as directed on each piece.

Step 2. Cut nine 8¹/₂" x 30" pieces freezer paper. Fold each section into quarters along the length to prepare a four-layer stack. Trim photocopied block diagrams, leaving a narrow margin around outer lines.

Step 3. Position one block copy on top of the stack; staple once through the center of each foundation shape. Carefully cut stack exactly splitting printed lines. Repeat with eight stacks.

Step 4. For half-blossom units, cut freezer-paper layers of remaining stack along dashed dividing line to yield half-B petals and half-A hexagons as shown in Figure 1.

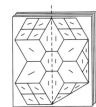

Figure 1
Cut freezer-paper layers of 1 stack along dashed dividing line to yield half-B petals and half-A hexagons.

Step 5. Cut remaining freezer paper into three 7¹/₈" x 18" pieces; fold in quarters, layer each with one photocopy of D and one border foundations diagram and staple. Carefully cut out all shapes, cutting D on inner seam line.

Step 6. Remove staples and separate freezer-paper shapes as needed. *Note: Retain copy-paper shapes and use glue stick to attach for foundation piecing, as needed.*

Making Blossoms

Step 1. For each whole blossom, iron-fuse plastic side of freezer-paper shapes onto the backside of six B petals and one A center patch. Prepare fabric shapes by folding seam allowance exactly at paper edges and basting all around. At B narrow tip, allow excess seam allowance tail to extend beyond folded edge. *Note: Tails will eventually be hidden behind adjacent patchwork.* Join petals to center A hexagon and adjacent petal edges to complete one blossom unit as shown in Figure 2; press. Complete 31 whole blossoms.

Figure 2
Join petals to center A hexagon and adjacent petal edges to complete 1 whole blossom.

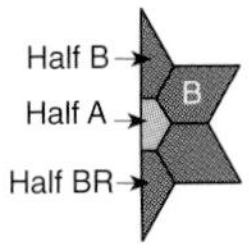

Figure 3
Join petals to half A and to adjacent petal edges.

Step 2. Follow same preparation as in Step 1 with two whole B petals, one half-B petal, one half-BR petal and one half-A hexagon. *Note: The seam allowances along dashed edge of half shapes remain flat and unbasted. These will be caught in side border seams later.* Join petals to half A and to adjacent petal edges as shown in Figure 3 to complete a half-blossom unit; press. Complete eight half blossoms.

Making Filler Diamonds

Step 1. For each filler diamond, iron-fuse paper shapes onto two rust stripe and two tan floral C diamonds. Fold seam allowance at paper edges as for other shapes in previous steps. At narrow diamond tips, allow excess seam allowance tails to extend beyond diamond shape. *Note: Tails will be hidden behind adjacent patchwork.*

Step 2. Join diamonds in two rows; then join rows as shown in Figure 4; press. Repeat for 92 filler diamonds.

Figure 4
Join diamonds in 2 rows;
then join rows as shown
for filler diamonds.

Figure 5
Join half-C diamonds to
adjacent rust C diamond sides
to make half-filler diamonds.

Making Half-Filler Diamonds

Step 1. For each half-filler diamond, follow same process as for filler diamonds with one rust stripe A and two tan floral half-C diamonds. *Note: The seam allowances along half-diamond long edges remain flat and unbasted. These will be caught in side border seams later.* Join half-C diamonds to adjacent rust C diamond sides as shown in Figure 5; press. Repeat for 26 half-filler diamonds.

Center Assembly

Step 1. Prepare row 1 by alternating and joining four whole blossoms and five filler diamonds with one half blossom on each end as shown in Figure 6.

Figure 6
Alternate and join 4 whole blossoms
and 5 filler diamonds with 1 half
blossom on each end for row 1.

Step 2. Join 10 filler diamonds along lower edge of row 1 blossoms between petal points as shown in Figure 7.

Figure 7
Join 10 filler diamonds along lower edge
of row 1 blossoms between petal points.

Step 3. Prepare row 2 by alternating and joining five whole blossoms and four filler diamonds with one half-filler diamond on each end as shown in Figure 8; align corresponding edges of rows 1 and 2 and join.

Figure 8
Prepare row 2 by alternating and joining
5 whole blossoms and 4 filler diamonds
with 1 half-filler diamond on each end.

Step 4. Repeat Step 2 for lower edge of row 2 as shown in Figure 9.

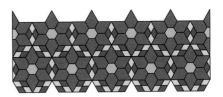

Figure 9
Add 10 filler diamonds to
the lower edge of row 2.

Step 5. Repeat Step 1 for rows 3, 5 and 7; repeat Step 3 for rows 4 and 6. Repeat Step 2 between each blossom row as shown in Figure 10.

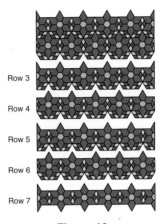

Figure 10
Add rows 3–7 with 10 filler
diamonds between rows.

Step 6. Iron-fuse freezer-paper D shapes onto the wrong side of 10 D fabric patches.

Step 7. Prepare shapes by folding seam allowance over both short edges only. *Note: Long edge remains flat and unbasted. It will be caught in upper or lower border seams later.*

Step 8. Join one half-filler diamond to each basted edge of D to make a D unit as shown in Figure 11; press.

Figure 11
Join 1 half-filler diamond unit to each
basted edge of D to make a D unit.

Step 9. Align and join prepared D units in spaces between blossom petal points at panel upper and lower edges to square up edges as shown in Figure 12.

Figure 12
Align and join prepared D units in spaces
between blossom petal points at panel
upper and lower edges to square up edges.

Step 10. Working from the wrong side of the pieced top, use rotary cutter and ruler to trim excess seam allowance to ¼" beyond exposed edges of paper foundations on all four sides.

Adding Borders

Note: The character of English paper-foundation piecing may require slight adjustments in lengths of borders. Verify center panel edge measurements, then cut the following border strips, adjusting sizes as necessary.

Step 1. Cut two 2" x 40½" E strips and two 3" x 45¼" F strips tan floral. Sew F to opposite long sides and E to the top and bottom of the pieced center; press seams toward strips.

Step 2. Prepare C pieces with freezer paper as for pieces A and B. Prepare fabric shapes by folding seam allowance exactly at paper edges and basting all around, allowing tails to extend naturally. ***Note:*** *Seam allowances of half- and quarter-C pieces that will lie at section edges or ends remain flat and unbasted.*

Step 3. Join one rust stripe C and two tan floral C pieces to make C units as shown in Figure 13; repeat for 34 units. Prepare four end units as shown in Figure 14. Join 17 C units and two end units to make a row as shown in Figure 15; repeat for two rows.

Figure 13
Join 1 rust stripe C and 2 tan floral half-C pieces to make C units.

Figure 14
Prepare 4 end units.

Figure 15
Join 17 C units and 2 end units to make a row.

Step 4. Cut four 1½" x 1⅝" G pieces tan floral. Sew G to each end of each C row as shown in Figure 16.

Figure 16
Sew G to each end of each C row.

Step 5. Sew a C row to the top and bottom of the center panel. ***Note:*** *If necessary, trim excess seam allowance to ¼" beyond exposed paper foundations on all edges of each pieced border section before sewing to the center panel.*

Step 6. Cut two 1⅞" x 40½" H strips tan floral. Sew

Star Flowers
Placement Diagram
Approximately 54" x 66¾"

a strip to the top and bottom of the center panel; press seams toward H.

Step 7. Cut and piece two 1½" x 53¼" I and two 1½" x 42½" J strips rust mottled. Sew I to opposite long sides and J to the top and bottom of the center panel; press seams toward I and J.

Step 8. Cut and piece two 6½" x 55¼" K and two 6½" x 54½" L strips teal stripe. Sew K to opposite long sides and L to the top and bottom of the center panel; press seams toward L and K.

FINISHING THE QUILT

Step 1. Mark quilting lines as desired.

Step 2. Sandwich thin cotton batting between the completed quilt top and prepared backing piece; pin or baste layers together to hold.

Step 3. Quilt on marked lines. When quilting is complete, remove pins or basting.

Step 4. Trim excess batting and backing even with quilt top.

Step 5. Prepare a 255" length of 2¼"-wide teal stripe bias binding and apply to quilt edges to finish. ❖

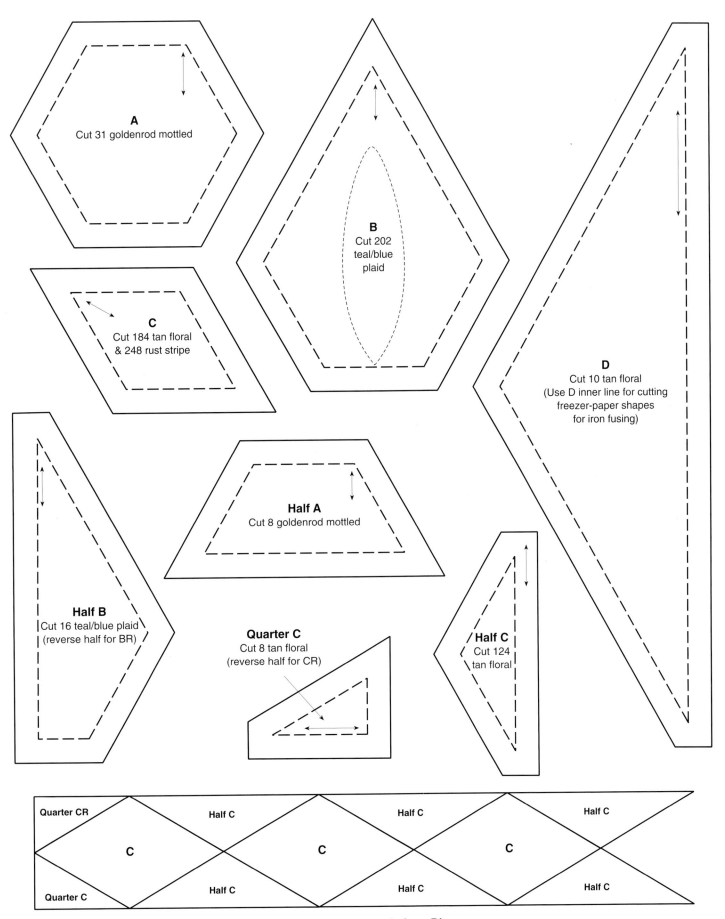

A
Cut 31 goldenrod mottled

B
Cut 202 teal/blue plaid

C
Cut 184 tan floral & 248 rust stripe

D
Cut 10 tan floral
(Use D inner line for cutting freezer-paper shapes for iron fusing)

Half A
Cut 8 goldenrod mottled

Half B
Cut 16 teal/blue plaid
(reverse half for BR)

Quarter C
Cut 8 tan floral
(reverse half for CR)

Half C
Cut 124 tan floral

Quarter CR	Half C		Half C		Half C
C		C		C	
Quarter C	Half C		Half C		Half C

Border Diamonds Foundations Diagram
Make 3 photocopies, layer with freezer paper, then cut shapes for piecing.

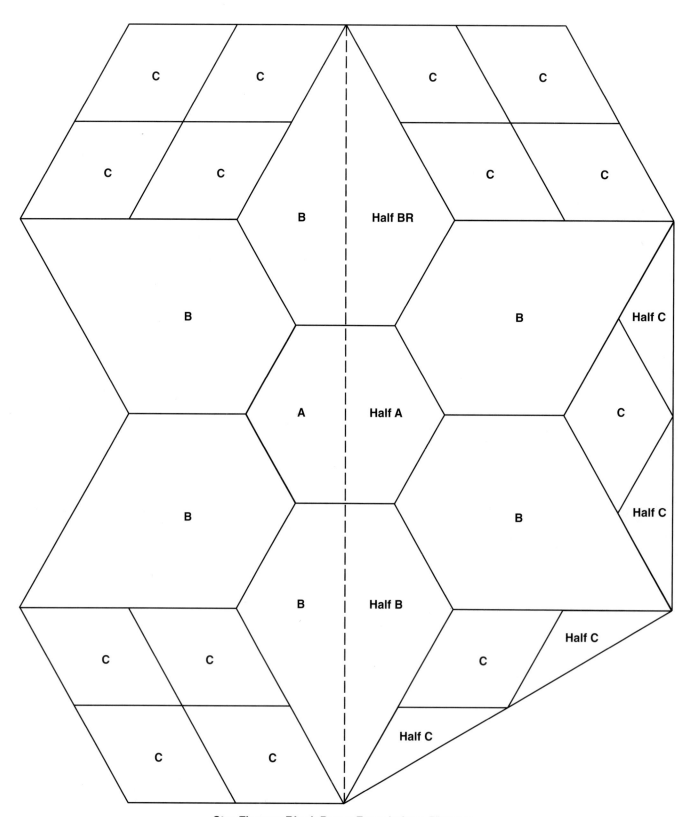

Star Flowers Block Paper-Foundations Diagram
Make 9 photocopies, layer with freezer paper, then cut shapes for piecing.

Hexagon Piecing
With Reusable Foundations

Reusable, purchased foundation pieces help make the stitching process quick and easy.

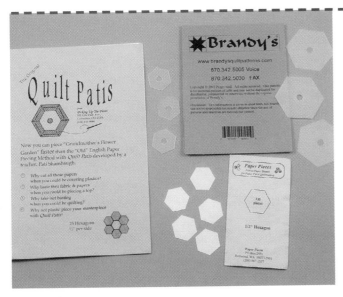

1

FUSSY CUTTING SHAPES

1A. Alternatives to photocopied standard-weight paper or freezer-paper foundation shapes are many reusable, precut, heavier-weight card stock, plastic or Mylar shapes available commercially. Many typical shapes and a variety of sizes are available. Card-stock shapes are penetrable enough to allow basting through the shape as is done with regular paper shapes. They will retain shape and strength for at least two or three repeated uses. For more rigid materials, slight modifications to the foundation preparation and joining process should be used.

1B. If purchased shapes are not available, prepare a hexagon template with a window cut out to represent the finished size of the shape to be fussy cut, in this case a star.

1C. Secure plastic or Mylar reusable foundation shape with a pin through the punched hole in the center. Fold seam allowance over in the same way that paper foundations are used. Tie on and anchor corner folds by taking two stitches through all seam allowance layers at each corner. Remove pin when several corners are complete and shape will remain in place without assistance. Tie off with a double stitch in place at final corner.

Tip
Prepare this template before shopping to audition a star print that will produce the flag effect.

Tip
This stitching is permanent and remains in place to help retain the shape even after foundation is removed. Use thread that matches fabric to avoid shadowing. Note: The photo uses a contrasting thread for visibility.

2

STITCHING UNITS TOGETHER

2A. Projects using rigid, resuable shapes are typically joined in rows. Prepare the first row by joining hexagons side by side, stitching on the side edges. Remaining rows are fitted into angles of the previous row and stitched to each adjacent patch.

2B. Once the adjacent row is complete, plastic shapes are removed. Flex the fabric shape and thread ring slightly to allow one edge to slip out from seam allowance; then remove.

2C. As with other foundation materials, change thread color so that it matches the color of at least one of the patches being joined. When the continuous seam will involve joining some mixed-color seams as well as same-color seams, select a thread color to match most of the patches. In this image, red is used because a red-to-red seam will continue after the red-to-blue stitching is complete.

2D. Rigid shapes will not crease opposite the currently aligned edges as paper does. Instead, edges being joined may need to be whipstitched in nearly flat positions. For larger plastic or Mylar shapes, it may be possible to flex and curl the work to allow a more normal, layered positioning of edges for stitching.

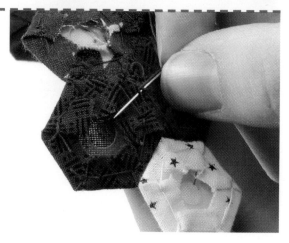

44 *Master Quilter's Workshop*

Old Glory Waving Wall Quilt

Watch the stars and stripes grow from left to right in this patriotic wall quilt.

PROJECT SPECIFICATIONS

Skill Level: Beginner

Quilt Size: Approximately 26¼" x 23¾"

MATERIALS

- 4 squares 1½" x 1½" red print for F
- 7" x 11" scrap each 7 red and 6 cream prints
- Scraps navy and medium blue wool felt for letters and stars
- 7" x 8" scrap blue solid
- ⅛ yard brown solid for narrow border
- ¼ yard blue-with-cream star for fussy-cutting hexagon patches
- ½ yard red/beige stripe for binding
- ½ yard golden beige solid or tone-on-tone for border
- Thin cotton batting 31" x 26"
- Backing 31" x 26"
- Neutral color all-purpose thread
- Contrasting quilting thread
- Ecru wool floss
- Fabric glue stick
- 1 card-stock photocopy of letter and star shapes to cut apart for tracing template
- 26 plastic or Mylar ½" reusable hexagons (or substitute 16 copies of the Season's Splendor Hexagon Master on page 31)
- Basic sewing tools and supplies, water-erasable marker or pencil and template material

PROJECT NOTES

Try using precut plastic or Mylar hexagons to eliminate cutting paper foundations. These are available in many sizes and are purchased in packages of multiples of one size.

Refer to Hexagon Piecing With Reusable Foundations on page 41 for step-by-step photo illustrations.

INSTRUCTIONS

Patch Preparation & Joining

Step 1. Prepare hexagon template with interior hexagon window cut out as shown in Figure 1. Fussy-cut 50 hexagon patches with one star from the blue-with-cream star print centered in the window as shown in Figure 2. ***Note:** If using purchased Mylar or plastic templates, do not prepare template. Instead, center the hole in the template on a star and cut out patches. Purchased paper templates cannot be used for cutting in this manner, but can be used for the finishing process.*

Figure 1
Cut out interior hexagon window on template.

Figure 2
Center 1 star from the blue-with-cream star print in the window.

Step 2. Cut 16 matching blue solid hexagons.

Step 3. Determine the most pleasing alternating red and cream fabric order for 13 stripes. Create an order swatch card with top red row assigned number 1, through red row 13 at the bottom. Use hexagon template to cut the following: 11 red hexagon patches each for rows 1, 3 and 5; 22 red hexagon patches each for rows 7, 9, 11 and 13; 11 cream hexagon patches each for rows 2, 4 and 6; and 22 cream hexagon patches each for rows 8, 10 and 12.

Step 4. Prepare fabric-covered foundation shapes for the first vertical column forming the left edge of the flag panel. The column is made up of six blue solid and one red or cream each from rows 7 through 13. Join shapes side by side as shown in Figure 3.

Figure 3
Join shapes side by side.

Step 5. Prepare fabric-covered foundation shapes for second column: one blue solid, five blue-with-cream star print and one red or cream each from rows 7 through 13.

Step 6. Position and attach shapes in sequence, beginning with blue solid patch at the top, joined to bottom angled edge of top end blue solid hexagon from column 1 as

Figure 4
Position and attach shapes in sequence as shown.

Figure 5
Join subsequent patches to previous patch of the current column as well as adjacent patch from previous column.

shown in Figure 4.

Step 7. For each successive column, join the first patch to the previous column. Join subsequent patches to the previous patch of the current column as well as adjacent patch from previous column as shown in Figure 5. When the second column is complete, press and remove plastic or Mylar shapes for repeat use. *Note: If using paper shapes, leave in place until the entire panel is complete.*

Step 8. Prepare same fabric shapes as listed in Step 5. Position and attach as for column 2 except join patches to top angled edges of corresponding hexagons of previous column as shown in Figure 6.

Figure 6
Join patches to top angled edges of corresponding hexagons of previous column.

Step 9. Continue preparing and joining hexagon columns, alternating attachment to bottom or top angled edges of adjacent hexagons to form a waving effect. Complete 10 columns, continuing to repeat patch colors from column 2.

Flag Panel & Borders

Step 1. Release basting as needed at upper, lower and side edges to allow seam allowance to be unfolded and pressed

Figure 7
Release basting as needed at upper, lower and side edges to allow seam allowance to be unfolded and pressed flat.

flat as shown in Figure 7.

Step 2. To straight-trim side edges, place a rotary ruler with ¼" guideline along pieced panel at outer corners. Trim at ruler edge as shown in Figure 8; repeat for upper

Old Glory Waving Wall Quilt
Placement Diagram
26¼" x 23¾"

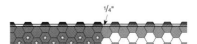

Figure 8
Place a rotary ruler with ¼" guideline along pieced panel at outer corners; trim at ruler edge.

Figure 9
Place the ¼" guideline along centers of extending hexagons; trim as shown.

and lower edges, placing ¼" guideline along centers of extending hexagons as shown in Figure 9.

Step 3. Cut two 2" x 11½" A strips and one strip each 2" x 19¾" (B) and one 4¾" x 19¾" (C) golden beige solid.

Step 4. Sew an A strip to opposite short sides of the pieced center panel; press seams toward A.

Step 5. Sew B to the top and C to the bottom of the pieced center panel; press seams toward strips.

Step 6. Cut two 1½" x 17¼" D strips and two 1½" x 19¾" E strips brown solid. Sew D to opposite sides of the center panel; press seams toward D.

Step 7. Sew an F square to each end of each E strip; press seams toward E. Sew an E-F strip to the top and bottom of the center panel.

Step 8. Cut two 3" x 19 1/4" G strips and two 3" x 26¾" H strips golden beige solid or tone-on-tone. Sew G to opposite sides and H to the top and bottom of the center panel; press seams away from G and H.

Appliqué Message

Step 1. Cut out card-stock photocopied letters and stars. Trace and cut each letter from navy wool felt and two

stars from medium blue wool felt.

Step 2. Transfer letter positions to the C border strip by aligning the centerline and seam guidelines on the pattern with the strip. Position cut letters and secure in place with fabric glue or basting stitches.

Step 3. Complete a buttonhole embroidery stitch around stars and letters using ecru wool floss.

Finishing the Quilt

Step 1. Transfer single-twist quilting design to borders A and B, nine tip-to-tip stars centered across each H border, six stars centered across each G border and wavy lines through the center of each cream hexagon stripe row. Mark straight lines along lower and right edge of star field and $1/4$" echo line in beige borders beyond flag panel seams.

Step 2. Sandwich thin cotton batting between the completed quilt top and prepared backing piece; pin or baste layers together to hold.

Step 3. Quilt in the ditch around flag panel edges, along inner edge of contrasting narrow borders, around stars and letters and on all marked lines using contrasting quilting thread.

Step 4. When quilting is complete, remove pins or basting; trim batting and backing edges with quilted top.

Step 5. Prepare 112" of $2^1/4$"-wide bias binding from red/ beige stripe and apply to edges to finish. ❖

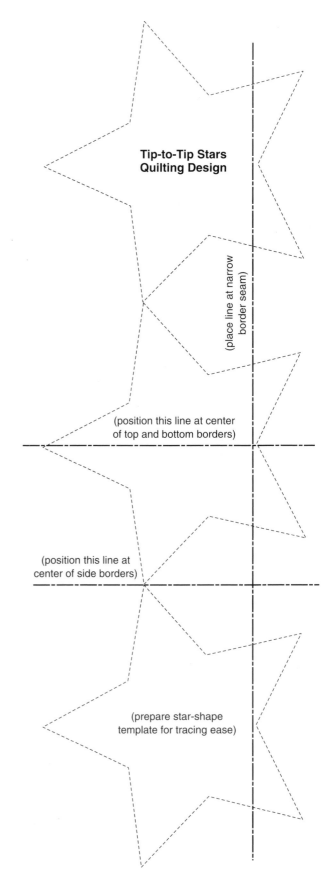

Tip-to-Tip Stars Quilting Design

(place line at narrow border seam)

(position this line at center of top and bottom borders)

(position this line at center of side borders)

(prepare star-shape template for tracing ease)

Centerline

(place this guideline along border seam)

(place this guideline along border seam)

Centerline

Letter Appliqué Pattern & Positions

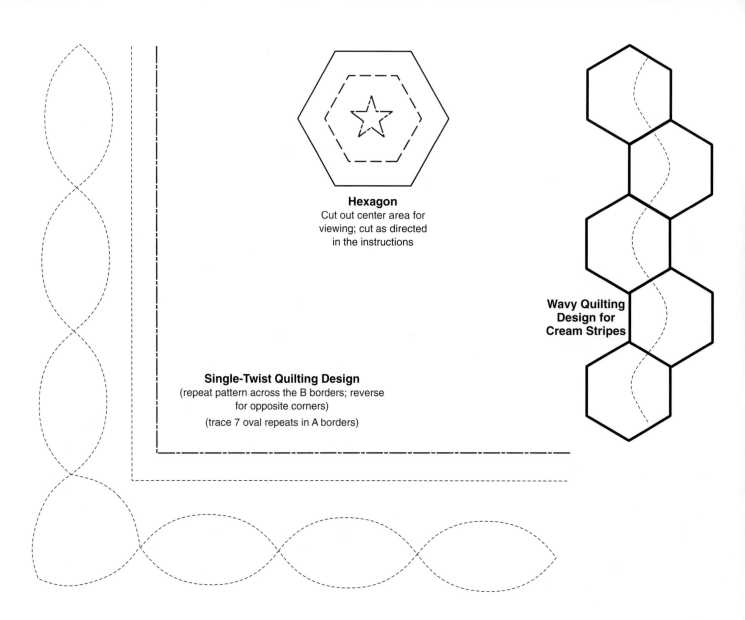

Hexagon
Cut out center area for
viewing; cut as directed
in the instructions

**Wavy Quilting
Design for
Cream Stripes**

Single-Twist Quilting Design
(repeat pattern across the B borders; reverse
for opposite corners)
(trace 7 oval repeats in A borders)

Piecing Diamonds

Refer to the step-by-step photos to aid in piecing Aunt Seph's Recipe.

1

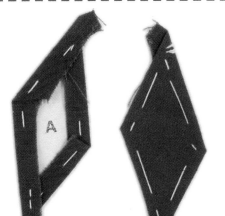

PREPARING DIAMOND SHAPES

1A. Secure paper diamonds against the backside of the fabric patch; fold and baste seam allowances snugly around shape. Allow tails to extend beyond folded edge of prepared diamond shape.

2

JOINING DIAMOND SHAPES

2A. Begin star unit by joining A and AR (A reversed) diamond pairs with long edge at center.

Tip
Rotate extending tails so that they radiate in the same direction. This will reduce the interference between tails of adjacent diamond patches.

2B. Prepare star unit using eight diamond patches.

Front   Back

Tip
Reduce bulk at star center by trimming away excess seam allowance tails.

2C. Continue assembly of Yankee Pride pieced appliqué, finally adding blossoms next to partial stars.

3

MAKING LOVER'S KNOT UNITS

3A. Join four F arc shapes to a background E shape to complete a Lover's Knot unit.

Front   Back

3B. Join F arc edges to curved edges of background G creating the foundation for appliqués with openings.

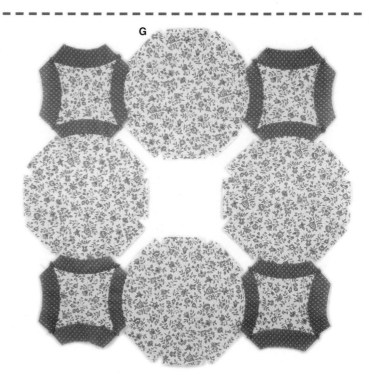

APPLIQUÉ

4A. Position Yankee Pride appliqué over opening, aligning folded edges with traced temporary guidelines on G. Pin to secure; appliqué in place.

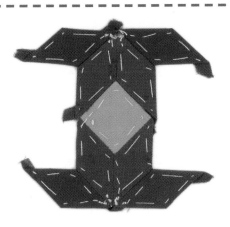

4B. Prepare double blossom units as shown. These are positioned over openings of Lover's Knot units around edges of center panel.

Aunt Seph's Recipe

Two traditional patchwork designs, Yankee Pride and Lover's Knot, are paired to form a lattice pattern. This unique combination and its title commemorate a country woman's down-home ingenuity in whipping up something wonderful from what she had on hand.

PROJECT SPECIFICATIONS

Skill Level: Advanced

Quilt Size: 83$\frac{1}{2}$" x 102$\frac{1}{2}$"

MATERIALS

- $\frac{3}{4}$ yard rust solid
- 1$\frac{1}{4}$ yards goldenrod solid
- 2$\frac{1}{2}$ yards medium blue pin dot
- 4$\frac{1}{2}$ yards dark blue solid
- 5$\frac{3}{4}$ yards white print
- Thin cotton batting 90" x 109"
- Backing 90" x 109"
- Neutral color all-purpose thread
- Contrasting quilting thread
- Fabric glue stick
- 10$\frac{1}{2}$ yards $\frac{1}{8}$" poly cord for piping
- Paper for foundation piecing
- Basic sewing tools and supplies and water-erasable marker or pencil

PROJECT NOTES

The whole Yankee Pride design and the blossom portions of the Lover's Knot design are pieced then joined into one unit using English paper-foundation construction.

The arc center section of the Lover's Knot unit is pieced using traditional curved hand-piecing techniques, then joined to the corresponding curved edges of the background sections G, H or I. Temporary position guidelines are transferred to the right side of G, H and I, then foundation-pieced assemblies are positioned over the openings and stitched in place. Extra blossom units are added at side and top or bottom edges.

Larger arcs are pieced to corresponding background sections H and I. Border sections are joined in sequence to complete the panel. Contrast bias appliqué strips are then stitched next to J or K edges.

Tracing templates are shown without seam allowances added so that seam lines can be traced on the wrong side of the fabric for E, F, J, K, L and M or the right side of the fabric for G, H and I. Seam allowances of $\frac{1}{4}$" should be added when cutting.

INSTRUCTIONS

Making Yankee Pride Units

Step 1. Prepare templates for A, C and D using pattern pieces given; cut as directed on each piece. Set aside goldenrod C pieces for Lover's Knot units.

Step 2. Photocopy the master sheet as directed on the pattern. Cut photocopied A, AR, C and D foundation shapes exactly on printed lines. Secure each paper shape centered with unprinted side against the wrong side of the corresponding fabric patch as shown in Figure 1.

Figure 1
Secure each paper shape centered with unprinted side against the wrong side of the corresponding fabric patch.

Figure 2
Fold seam allowances exactly at paper shape edges; baste 1 edge at a time until all edges are prepared.

Step 3. Fold seam allowances exactly at paper shape edges; baste one edge at a time until all edges are prepared as shown in Figure 2. Allow tails at narrow A points to extend naturally beyond folded diamond shape.

Step 4. Join long edges of one dark blue A and one AR as shown in Figure 3; repeat for four A-AR units. Join two A-AR units to complete star halves; join halves to complete a star unit referring to Figure 4.

Figure 3
Join long edges of 1 dark blue A and 1 AR.

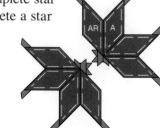

Figure 4
Join 2 A-AR units to complete star halves; join halves to complete a star unit.

Tip

Hold extending tails out of the way when joining shapes so that folded edges only can be pierced with needle and thread.

Step 5. Sew white print C and D squares between star points referring to Figure 5.

Figure 5
Sew C and D squares between star points.

Figure 6
Join 3 each dark blue A and AR pieces to form a partial star unit.

Step 6. Join three each dark blue A and AR pieces to form a partial star unit as shown in Figure 6; repeat for four units.

Step 7. Sew a partial star unit to a star unit at C intersections to complete a Yankee Pride unit as shown in Figure 7. Repeat to complete 32 Yankee Pride units.

Figure 7
Sew a partial star unit to a star unit at C intersections to complete a Yankee Pride unit.

Making Blossom Units

Step 1. Prepare template for B piece using the pattern given; cut as directed on the piece.

Step 2. Cut the photocopied B and BR foundation shapes exactly on printed lines. Secure each paper shape centered with unprinted side against the wrong side of the corresponding fabric patch. Prepare blossom units with one each rust B and BR and one each dark blue B and BR as shown in Figure 8; repeat for 156 B units. Set aside 14 B units.

Figure 8
Prepare blossom units with 1 each rust B and BR and 1 each dark blue B and BR.

Step 3. Set a goldenrod C square into the opening between the rust B and BR pieces to complete a blossom unit as shown in Figure 9. Repeat for 142 blossom units.

Figure 9
Set a goldenrod C square into the opening between the rust B and BR pieces to complete a blossom unit.

Joining Pieced Units

Step 1. Sew four blossom units to a Yankee Pride unit as shown in Figure 10; repeat with all Yankee Pride units.

Figure 10
Sew 4 blossom units to a Yankee Pride unit.

Step 2. Sew a B unit to a blossom unit as shown in Figure 11; repeat for 14 double blossom units.

Figure 11
Sew a B unit to a blossom unit to complete a double blossom unit.

Step 3. Prepare templates for E and F pieces using the tracing templates given. Cut as directed on each template, adding a 1/4" seam allowance all around when cutting fabric patches.

Step 4. Sew an F piece to each side of an E piece as shown in Figure 12 to make a Lover's Knot unit, matching center marks on E and F pieces; press seams toward F. Repeat for 31 Lover's Knot units.

Figure 12
Sew an F piece to each
side of an E piece.

Tip

Clip halfway into seam allowances at ¼" to ⅜" intervals along inside curved edges of E or F to ease seam alignment and stitching.

Join Pieced Units With Background Pieces

Step 1. Prepare templates for pieces G, H and I using tracing templates given. Trace outside edges of template to the right side of the fabrics for appliqué guidelines, then cut shapes, adding a ¼" seam allowance all around when cutting.

Step 2. Arrange G background pieces into eight rows of six pieces each. Rotate end pieces of rows 1 and 8 so that the partial star extension edges are facing the outer corner as shown in Figure 13. Position Lover's Knot units to correspond to curved edges of end G pieces as shown in Figure 14.

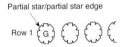

Figure 13
Rotate end G pieces of rows 1 and 8.

Figure 14
Position Lover's Knot units to correspond
to curved edges of end G pieces.

Step 3. Rotate adjacent G pieces so curved edges align with the Lover's Knot units and rotate G pieces to arrange entire panel interior as shown in Figure 15.

Step 4. Stitch corresponding G curved edges to the Lover's Knot units, matching center marks on F with mark on G. *Note: The G seam lines are marked on front side of G patches and F seam lines are marked on wrong side of F pieces.* Press seams toward F.

Step 5. Arrange H and HR pieces at panel edges with long curved edges away from panel and short curved edges

Figure 15
Rotate adjacent G pieces so curved edges
align with the Lover's Knot units and rotate
G to arrange entire panel interior.

corresponding to the unattached F edges of the Lover's Knot units as shown in Figure 16.

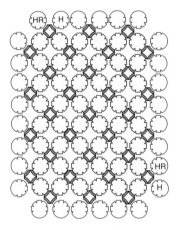

Figure 16
Arrange H and HR pieces at panel edges
with long curved edges away from panel and
short curved edges corresponding to the
unattached F edges of the Lover's Knot units.

Step 6. Stitch H curved edges to the Lover's Knot units as in Step 4; press seams toward F.

Step 7. Place one Yankee Pride/blossom unit over an opening in the center panel. Align edges exactly along traced guidelines with center seam of blossom units aligned with F ends as shown in Figure 17; pin to secure.

Tip

If appliqué unit seems slightly overlarge, ease appliqué to fit by compressing appliqué edges or slightly stretching background patches.

Figure 17
Align edges of units exactly along traced guidelines with center seam of blossom units aligned with F ends.

Step 8. Appliqué-stitch edges in place all around. Trim excess seam allowance tails at diamond tips, then neatly tuck behind appliqué edge referring to Figure 18; stitch precise points. Repeat for all 32 Yankee Pride units. *Note: For units at panel edges, leave the edges of the dark blue blossom diamonds unattached to allow for joining of border arcs.*

Figure 18
Trim excess seam allowance tails at diamond tips, then neatly tuck behind appliqué edge.

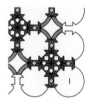

Figure 19
Position I background corner patch with Yankee Pride unit edges aligned at guidelines.

Step 9. Position I background corner patches with Yankee Pride unit edges aligned at guidelines as shown in Figure 19. Appliqué edges, leaving blossom dark blue diamonds at panel edge unattached.

Step 10. Align one end of each double blossom unit from Step 2 of Joining Pieced Units over the vacant Lover's Knot ends as shown in Figure 20. Appliqué only the edge that overlaps the arc ends.

Adding Borders

Step 1. Prepare templates for pieces J, K, L and M using tracing templates given; cut as directed on templates, adding a ¼" seam allowance all around each piece when

Aunt Seph's Recipe
Placement Diagram
83½" x 102½"

Figure 20
Align 1 end of each double blossom unit over the vacant Lover's Knot ends.

cutting. Transfer all marks to each fabric patch to assist with matching during the assembly process.

Step 2. Prepare a 13-yard length of 1¼"-wide bias from goldenrod solid. Fold in half along length with wrong sides together and press.

Step 3. Position the bias strip along the inner edge of each J and K piece with raw edges aligned; baste in place.

Step 4. Sew J to L and K to M as shown in Figure 21; press seams toward L and M. Hand-stitch bias edge in place on J and K pieces.

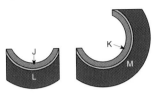

Figure 21
Sew J to L and K to M.

Step 5. Keeping blossom ends out of the way, sew a J-L border unit to H and K-M corner units to I; press seams toward border pieces.

Step 6. Join adjacent border-unit seams, stopping and locking stitches at scallop edges as marked with a dot on the template.

Step 7. Reposition the free blossom ends so that outside dark blue diamond edges overlap arc ends; appliqué remaining edges to complete the top.

Step 8. Remove all basting and foundation papers.

Finishing the Quilt

Step 1. Transfer quilting designs to the center of the Lover's Knot E units, to G, H and I background sections and to the full and partial stars in the Yankee Pride units. Mark ¼" echo lines beyond appliquéd edges in all large background sections and inside golden-rod C squares

and echo lines 1" and 2" from goldenrod trim in dark blue border.

Step 2. Sandwich thin cotton batting between the completed quilt top and prepared backing piece; pin or baste layers together to hold.

Step 3. Quilt on marked lines and in the ditch of seams around patchwork using contrasting quilting thread.

Step 4. When quilting is complete, remove pins or basting; trim batting and backing edges with quilted top.

Step 5. Prepare a 10¼-yard length of ⅞"-wide bias from medium blue pin dot. Fold around the ⅛" poly cord and stitch close to cord to make piping. Apply piping to quilt top and batting edges, keeping backing edge free. Fold top/piping edges under; fold backing seam allowance under and hand-stitch in place along piping seam as shown in Figure 22. *Note: Clip to seam line at inside angles between scallops to allow edge to be smoothly turned under.* ❖

Figure 22
Fold backing seam allowance under and hand-stitch in place along piping seam.

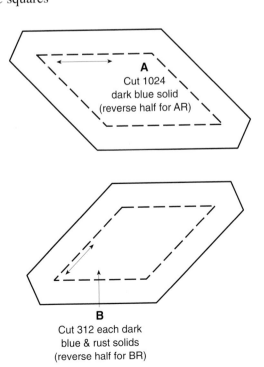

A
Cut 1024
dark blue solid
(reverse half for AR)

B
Cut 312 each dark
blue & rust solids
(reverse half for BR)

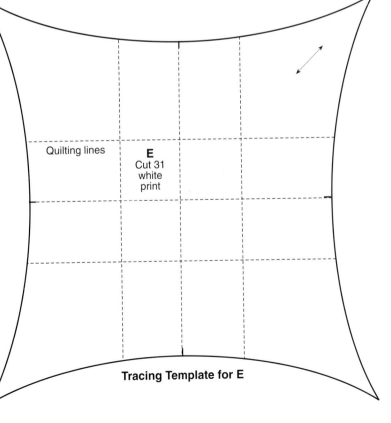

Quilting lines

E
Cut 31
white
print

Tracing Template for E

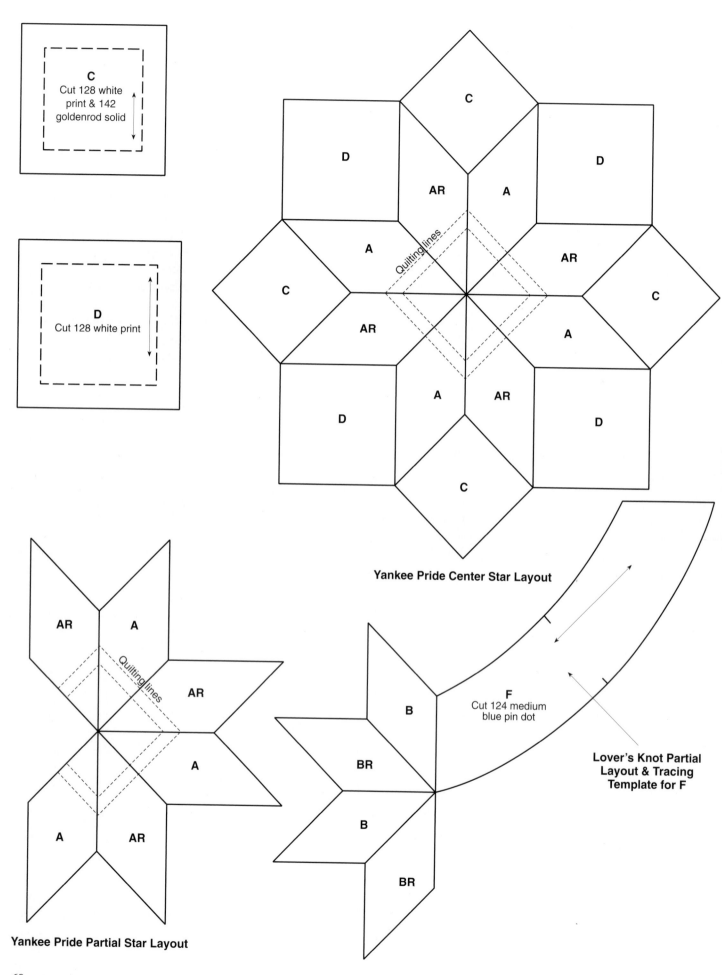

C
Cut 128 white print & 142 goldenrod solid

D
Cut 128 white print

Quilting lines

C

D

AR

A

A

AR

C

C

AR

A

AR

A

D

C

D

Yankee Pride Center Star Layout

AR

A

AR

A

A

AR

Quilting lines

F
Cut 124 medium blue pin dot

B

BR

B

BR

Lover's Knot Partial Layout & Tracing Template for F

Yankee Pride Partial Star Layout

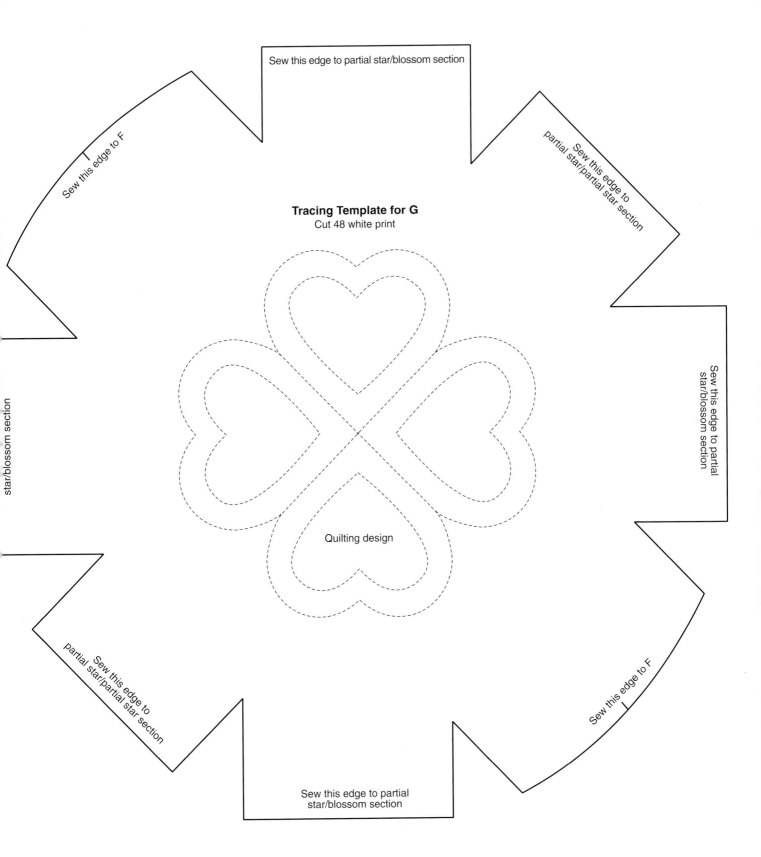

Sew this edge to partial star/blossom section

Sew this edge to F

Sew this edge to partial star/partial star section

Sew this edge to partial star/blossom section

star/blossom section

Tracing Template for G
Cut 48 white print

Quilting design

Sew this edge to partial star/partial star section

Sew this edge to F

Sew this edge to partial star/blossom section

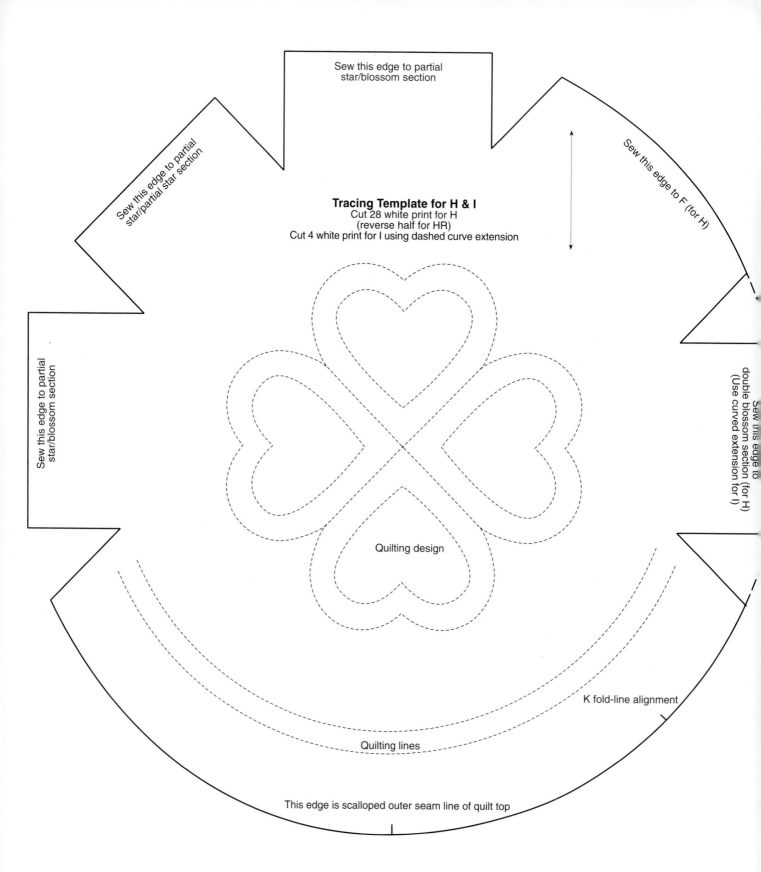

Sew this edge to partial
star/blossom section

Sew this edge to partial
star/partial star section

Sew this edge to F (for H)

Sew this edge to partial
star/blossom section

Sew this edge to
double blossom section (for H)
(Use curved extension for I)

Tracing Template for H & I
Cut 28 white print for H
(reverse half for HR)
Cut 4 white print for I using dashed curve extension

Quilting design

K fold-line alignment

Quilting lines

This edge is scalloped outer seam line of quilt top

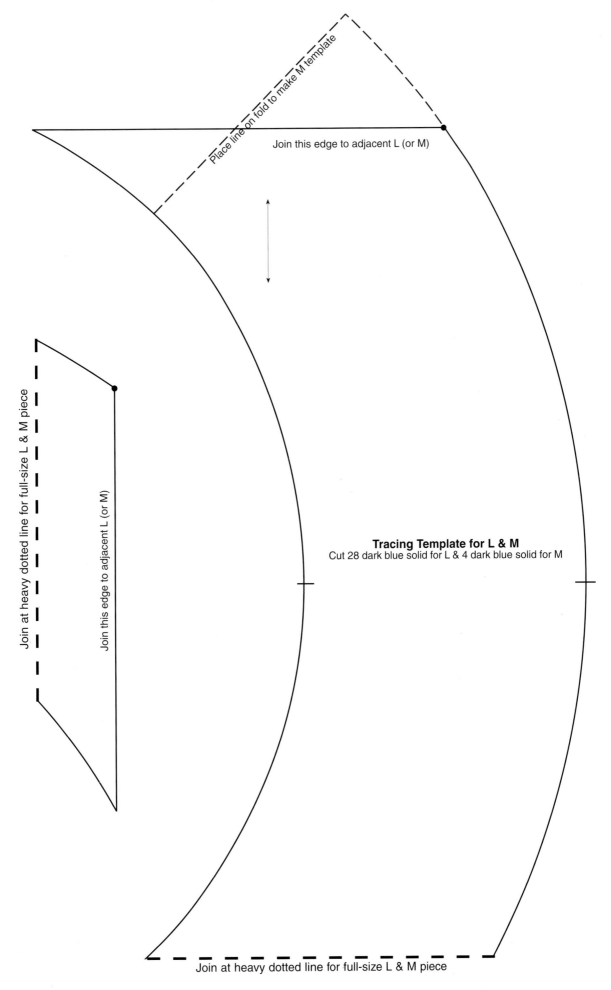

Place line on fold to make M template

Join this edge to adjacent L (or M)

Join at heavy dotted line for full-size L & M piece

Join this edge to adjacent L (or M)

Tracing Template for L & M
Cut 28 dark blue solid for L & 4 dark blue solid for M

Join at heavy dotted line for full-size L & M piece

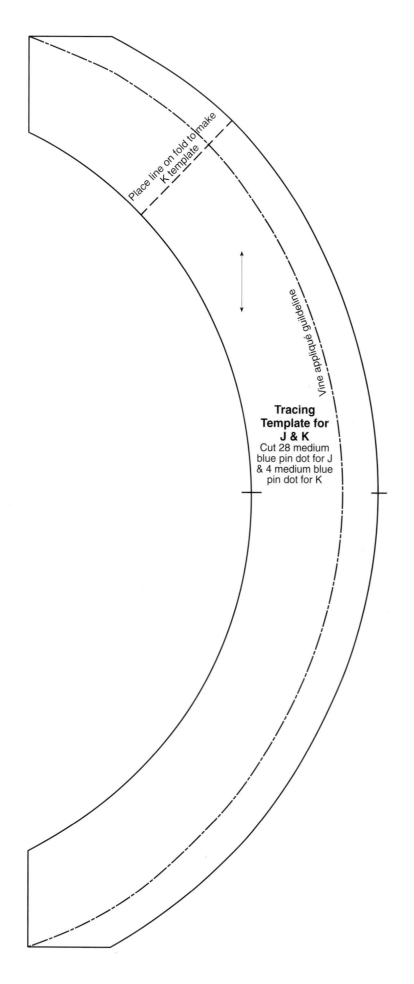

Place line on fold to make K template

Vine appliqué guideline

Tracing Template for J & K
Cut 28 medium blue pin dot for J & 4 medium blue pin dot for K

Make 32 copies of AR section. Cut shapes apart as needed exactly on lines.

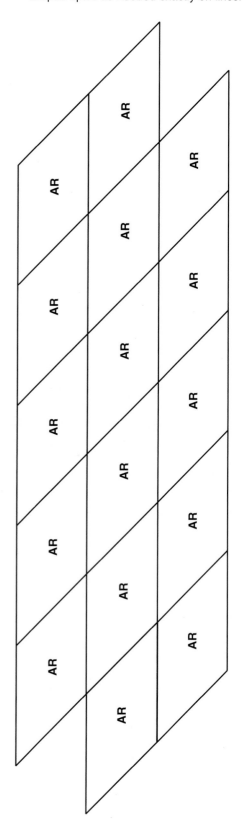

English Paper-Foundation Shapes Photocopy Master Sheet

Make 32 copies of this complete sheet and 7 extra copies of B and BR sections only. Cut shapes apart as needed exactly on lines.

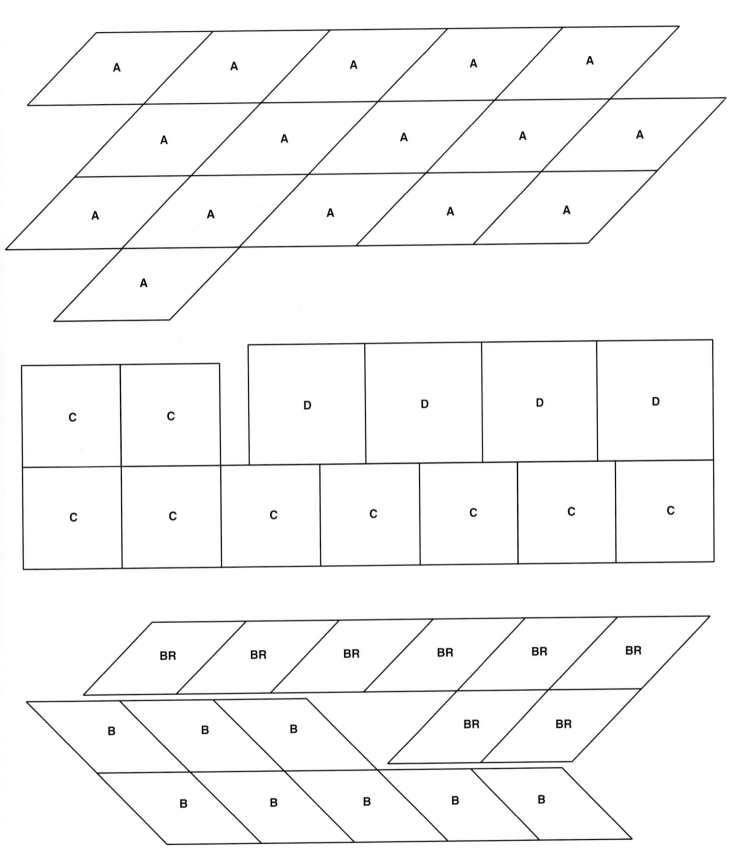

Appliqué Stitching Jewel-Shape Points

Appliqué shapes prepared as joined English-paper-foundation patchwork can be easily stitched to a background. Triangle, diamond and jewel shapes are slightly more difficult to apply than hexagons because of the seam allowance tails.

APPLIQUÉING POINTS

1A. To appliqué points, position shape and allow tails to extend naturally from behind shape. Trim excess tail tip to reduce bulk.

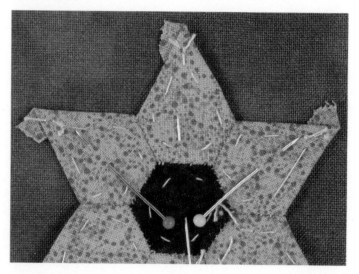

1B. Complete stitching along approaching point side to tip. Secure tip in position with an extra stitch. If tail lies in the way of stitching first edge, fold it out of the way.

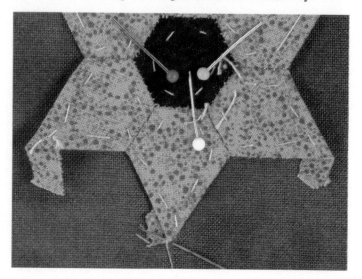

1C. Push tail under shape tip with needle point. Complete appliqué stitching along remaining tip edge to enclose tail.

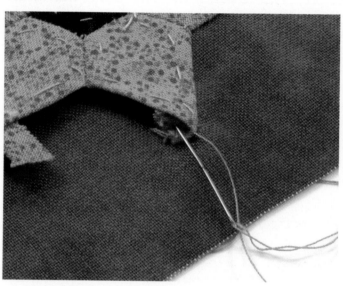

PREPARING SEPARATE PILLOW

2A. Prepare a separate sand pillow to secure sand at cube bottom portion. After cube is firmly stuffed with polyester fiberfill, the sand pillow is inserted in the remaining space, and the bottom seam is completed by hand.

Sunflower Pin Cube

Yellow-petal sunflowers on scrappy unequal-quarter backgrounds create a pretty pincushion.

PROJECT SPECIFICATIONS

Skill Level: Intermediate

Cube Size: $3^7/_8$" x $3^3/_4$" x $3^3/_4$"

MATERIALS

- Scraps of 17 coordinating brown fabrics, 5 golden-rod/yellow prints, black solid, dark rust solid and tan print
- $^1/_4$ yard muslin
- Thin cotton batting 5" x 27"
- Neutral color all-purpose thread
- Contrasting quilting thread
- Fabric glue stick
- Clear sandbox sand for weight
- Polyester fiberfill
- Basic sewing tools and supplies, water-erasable marker or pencil, and template material

INSTRUCTIONS

Sunflower Construction

Step 1. Make five photocopies of the Foundation Pattern; cut out each shape.

Step 2. Prepare F and G templates using patterns given. Cut pieces as directed on each piece.

Step 3. Glue-stick the paper shapes onto the wrong side of each fabric patch. Fold seam allowances over paper edges precisely and baste in place.

Step 4. Join six G pieces and one F piece to make a sunflower as shown in Figure 1; repeat for five sunflower units. *Note: Allow the seam allowance tails at the narrow tip of each jewel shape to extend naturally beyond the previous folded edge.*

Figure 1
Join 6 G pieces
and 1 F piece to
make a sunflower.

Cube Side Construction

Step 1. Cut two $4^1/_4$" x $4^1/_4$" A squares from one brown scrap; set aside.

Step 2. Prepare templates for pieces B–E and the Cube Cutting Template.

Step 3. Organize selected scraps into groups of four for each of the four cube sides, assigning and stacking each for specific B–E position. According to organized stacks, cut four patches with each template B–E.

Step 4. Join one each B, C, D and E piece to complete one cube side as shown in Figure 2; press. Repeat for four cube sides. Trim to size by centering Cube Cutting Template over each cube side, tracing lines and rotary-trimming on traced lines. *Note: Since the intersection of patchwork center seams will be covered by sunflower appliqués, seam lines do not need to be perfectly matched.*

Figure 2
Join 1 each B, C, D
and E pieces to
complete 1 cube side.

Completing Side Panels

Step 1. Cut four ⅝" x 4¼" H strips black solid; sew an H strip to the D/E edge of each cube side as shown in Figure 3; press seams toward H.

Figure 3
Sew an H strip to the D/E
edge of each cube side.

Step 2. Cut one 1" x 17" J strip each from tan print and dark rust solid. Join the strips with right sides together along length; press seams toward rust strip.

Step 3. Subcut strip set into sixteen 1" J segments as shown in Figure 4.

Figure 4
Subcut strip
set into sixteen
1" J segments.

Figure 5
Join 4 segments
to make a J strip.

Step 4. Join four J segments to make a J strip as shown in Figure 5; repeat for four J strips.

Step 5. Center and sew a J strip to the H side of each cube side; trim excess even with cube sides to complete the side panels as shown in Figure 6.

Figure 6
Sew a J strip to the H side
of each cube side to
complete the side panels.

Tip

To make it easier to work with narrow borders, they may be cut ¾"–1" wide, stitched in place and pressed. Use a rotary cutter and ruler and trim to ⅜".

Sunflower Appliqué

Step 1. Center a pieced sunflower unit on each side panel referring to the layout diagram for positioning; pin or baste in place.

Step 2. Appliqué in place, trimming excess tail seam allowances at petal tips as necessary. Fold tail out of the way to appliqué, then push tail under appliqué shape tip with needle to stitch tip in place.

Step 3. Cut away excess fabric from behind appliquéd sunflower shapes.

Step 4. Center and appliqué one sunflower unit to one A square for cube top as in Steps 2 and 3.

Finishing and Cube Assembly

Step 1. Join four cube side panels into one flat panel as shown in Figure 7, stopping and locking stitching at ¼" seam line at each end of seam; press seams open.

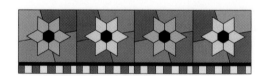

Figure 7
Join 4 cube side panels into 1 flat panel.

Step 2. Cut one 5" x 17" rectangle and two 5" x 5" squares each muslin for backing and thin cotton batting. Layer joined side panel and separate top and bottom A squares with batting and backing; pin or baste layers to hold.

Step 3. Machine-quilt around sunflower edges, next to border and checker seams and randomly meander over background areas using contrasting quilting thread.

Step 4. When quilting is complete, remove pins or basting; trim edges even.

Step 5. Clip at seam ends through batting and backing to match unstitched portion of seams.

Step 6. Join final side-to-side seam to form a tube, locking stitching as in Step 1. Pin, then join all four edges of sunflower A square, stopping and locking stitching at 1/4" seam lines at each corner.

Step 7. Pin, then join three edges of the bottom A square, leaving one side open to allow for stuffing; turn right side out.

Tip

Mark seam end dots on the wrong side of each quilted panel at seam to assist with positioning and joining of cube end squares.

Step 8. Stuff cube firmly with polyester fiberfill, leaving a scant 1" of depth unfilled near cube bottom.

Inner Cube Weight Pillow

Step 1. To prepare pillow, cut two 4 1/4" x 4 1/4" squares and one 1 1/2" x 15 1/2" strip muslin.

Step 2. Stay-stitch along long edges of the 1 1/2"-wide strip on the 1/4" seam line.

Step 3. Fold the strip to find and mark center on both edges, then measure and mark corner positions 3 3/4" and 7 1/2" on each side of the center as shown in Figure 8. Clip through seam allowance almost to stitching at each mark. Join short ends of strip to form a tube, stopping and locking stitching at stay-stitched ends of seam. Pin, then join all four edges of one 4 1/4" x 4 1/4" square to one edge of muslin tube, stopping and locking stitching at 1/4" seam lines at each marked corner.

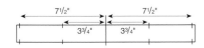

Figure 8
Fold the strip to find and mark center on both edges; measure and mark corner positions 3 3/4" and 7 1/2" on each side of the center.

Step 4. Pin, then join three edges of the remaining muslin square to remaining edge of tube. Leave a 2" opening on the final side at center for filling. Turn pillow right side out and fill with sand; hand-stitch opening securely closed.

Step 5. Insert sand pillow into bottom of stuffed cube. Fold under seam allowance of final cube bottom edge. Position and pin along corresponding cube side edge. Hand-stitch folded edge in place. ❖

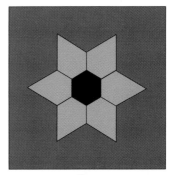

Top

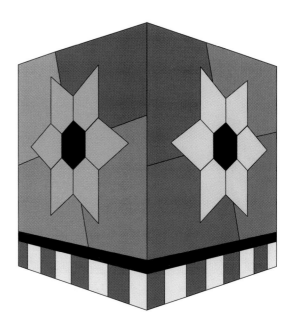

Sunflower Pin Cube
Placement Diagram
3 7/8" x 3 3/4" x 3 3/4"

Tips

To ensure that corner stitching leaves no gaps to allow sand leakage, stitch at an angle across corner seam allowances where seam lines cross after all seams are stitched.

To convert the pin cube into a door stop, prepare a wide liner pillow (or one that matches cube dimensions completely), then fill with sand and insert it inside the cube in place of the polyester fiberfill. Close openings securely to prevent sand leakage.

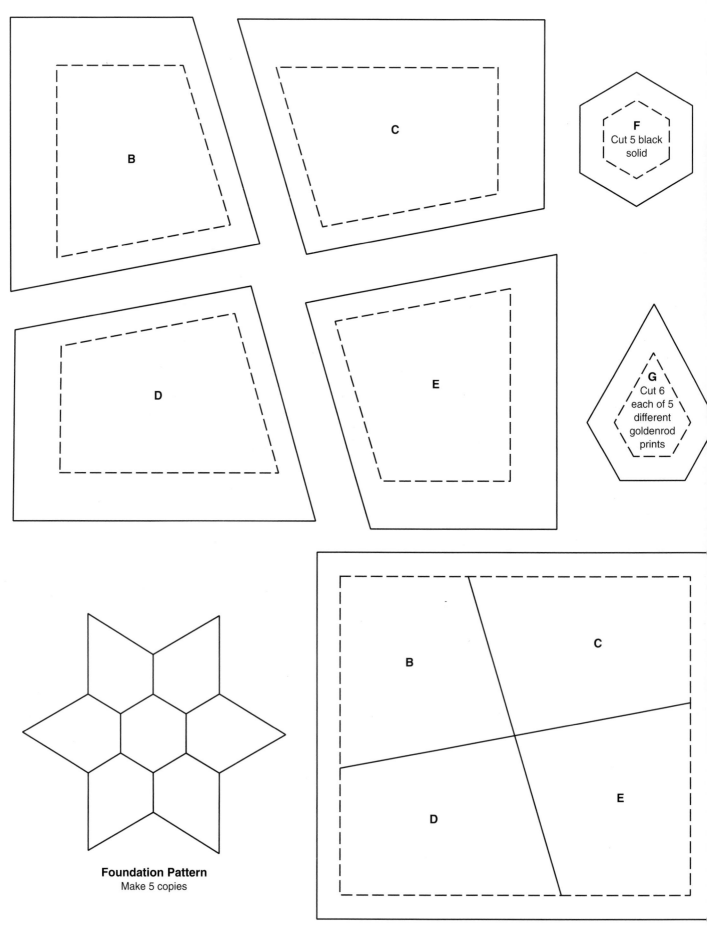

B

C

F
Cut 5 black
solid

D

E

G
Cut 6
each of 5
different
goldenrod
prints

Foundation Pattern
Make 5 copies

B

C

D

E

Cube Cutting Template

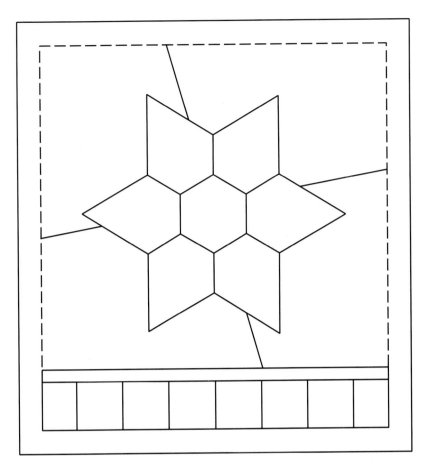

Cube Side Panel Layout

Petals & Posies

Hexagon posies team with Nine-Patch petals to make a cheery and colorful wall quilt.

PROJECT SPECIFICATIONS

Skill Level: Beginner

Quilt Size: 28" x 28"

Block Size: 6" x 6"

Number of Blocks: 9

MATERIALS

- Scraps medium green, light green and variegated dark peach
- $^1/_4$ yard orange dot
- $^1/_4$ yard yellow tone-on-tone
- $^5/_8$ yard fuchsia mottled
- $^7/_8$ yard navy mottled
- Thin cotton batting 34" x 34"
- Backing 34" x 34"
- Neutral color all-purpose thread
- Contrasting quilting thread
- 14" x 20" rectangle freezer paper
- $3^3/_4$ yards narrow poly cord for edge piping
- Stapler and staple remover
- Basic sewing tools and supplies, water-erasable marker or pencil, and template material

INSTRUCTIONS

Making Posy Blocks

Step 1. Make two photocopies of the Foundation Diagram and Block Layout.

Step 2. Cut five freezer-paper squares 6" x 6". Layer each photocopied diagram with two or three layers of freezer paper with diagram on top. Staple through the center of each hexagon.

Step 3. Cut out foundation shapes and remove staples.

Step 4. Prepare template for A using pattern given; cut 30 fuchsia mottled and five variegated dark peach scrap A hexagons.

Step 5. Center and iron-fuse foundation shapes on the wrong side of each fabric patch. Fold seam allowances over foundation edges precisely and baste in place. ***Note:*** *Refer to English Paper Piecing for Hexagons on page 7.*

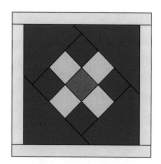

Petal
6" x 6" Block

Posy
6" x 6" Block

Step 6. Assemble five posies with variegated dark peach centers surrounded by six fuchsia mottled A hexagons to complete a posy motif as shown in Figure 1; press.

Figure 1
Join A hexagons as shown
to make a posy motif.

Step 7. Cut five $5^1/_2$" x $5^1/_2$" B squares navy mottled; fold and crease to mark center.

Tip

To compensate for potential take-up of block during the appliqué stitching, you may choose to cut the B squares 6" x 6" and then trim to size after posy motifs have been appliquéd in place. Be sure that the motif is centered when trimming.

Step 8. Center a prepared posy motif on the right side of a B square as shown in Figure 2; pin or baste in place to hold. Hand-stitch posy motif in place. Repeat for all blocks.

Figure 2
Center a prepared posy motif
on the right side of a B square.

Step 9. Carefully trim excess navy mottled away from behind appliquéd posy motifs from the wrong side of each square, leaving a $^1/_4$" seam allowance as shown in Figure 3.

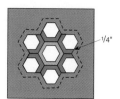

Figure 3
Trim excess navy mottled away from behind
appliquéd posy motifs from the wrong side of
each square, leaving a $^1/_4$" seam allowance.

Step 10. Remove basting and foundation papers.

Step 11. Cut six strips yellow tone-on-tone 1" by fabric width; subcut into 18 each 5½" C and 6½" D strips; set aside eight each C and D strips for Petal blocks.

Step 12. To complete the Posy blocks, sew a C strip to opposite sides and a D strip to the top and bottom of each posy unit as shown in Figure 4; press seams toward C and D strips.

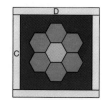

Figure 4
Sew a C strip to opposite
sides and a D strip to the top
and bottom of each posy unit.

Making Petal Blocks

Step 1. Cut two strips navy mottled (E) and one strip light green scrap (F) 1½" x 13". Sew the F strip between two E strips with right sides together along length to make a strip set; press seams toward E strips.

Step 2. Subcut strip set into 1½" segments as shown in Figure 5; you will need eight E-F segments.

Figure 5
Subcut strip set
into 1½" E-F
segments.

Step 3. Cut two strips light green scrap (G) and one strip medium green scrap (H) 1½" x 7". Sew the H strip between two G strips with right sides together along length to make a strip set; press seams toward the H strip.

Step 4. Subcut strip set into 1½" segments as shown in Figure 6; you will need four G-H segments.

Figure 6
Subcut strip set
into 1½" G-H
segments.

Figure 7
Sew a G-H segment
between 2 E-F segments
to make a Nine-Patch unit.

Step 5. Sew a G-H segment between two E-F segments to make a Nine-Patch unit as shown in Figure 7; press seams toward G-H. Repeat for four units.

Step 6. Cut eight 4" x 4" navy mottled J squares. Cut each

square in half on one diagonal to make triangles. Center and stitch the long edge of two triangles on opposite sides of each Nine-Patch unit as shown in Figure 8. *Note: Ends of triangles will extend beyond the edges of the Nine-Patch unit.* Press seams toward J.

Figure 8
Center and join the long edge
of 2 triangles on opposite
sides of each Nine-Patch unit.

Step 7. Trim edges of J triangles even with edges of the Nine-Patch unit as shown in Figure 9.

Figure 9
Trim edges of J triangles
even with edges of the
Nine-Patch unit.

Step 8. Center and sew a J triangle to the remaining two sides of each Nine-Patch unit; press seams toward J. Trim each unit to 5½" x 5½" using the Petal Block Trimming Template to center the Nine-Patch unit.

Tip

Trace the Petal Block Trimming Template onto see-through template material. Position the Nine-Patch area over corresponding seams of stitched unit. Mark template edge as a cutting line, then trim to 5½" finished size.

Step 9. To complete the Petal blocks, sew a C strip to opposite sides and a D strip to the top and bottom of each pieced unit as shown in Figure 10; press seams toward C and D strips.

Figure 10
Sew a C strip to opposite sides
and a D strip to the top and
bottom of each pieced unit.

Tip

Watch orientation of posy motifs as rows are assembled. Hexagon horizontal outer edges should be parallel to top and bottom of the quilt center.

Completing the Top

Step 1. Cut one 6½" by fabric width strip orange dot. Subcut strips into twenty-four 1¼" K sashing strips.

Step 2. Cut one 1¼" x 22" strip medium green scrap; subcut into sixteen 1¼" L sashing squares.

Step 3. Join two Posy blocks with one Petal block and four K strips to make a row referring to Figure 11; repeat for two rows. Press seams toward K.

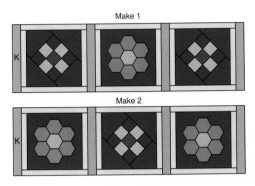

Make 1

Make 2

Figure 11
Join blocks with K strips to make a block row.

Step 4. Join two Petal blocks with one Posy block and four K strips to make a row, again referring to Figure 11; press seams toward K.

Step 5. Join three K strips and four L squares to make a sashing row as shown in Figure 12; repeat for four rows. Press seams toward K.

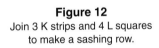

Figure 12
Join 3 K strips and 4 L squares
to make a sashing row.

Petals & Posies
Placement Diagram
28" x 28"

Step 6. Join the sashing rows with the block rows referring to the Placement Diagram for positioning; press seams toward sashing rows.

Step 7. Cut two 1" x 21½" M and two 1" x 22½" N strips fuchsia mottled. Sew M to opposite sides and N to the top and bottom of the pieced center; press seams toward strips.

Step 8. Cut four 4" x 31" O strips navy mottled; sew a strip to each side of the pieced center, mitering corners. Trim excess at miter and press seam open; press seams toward O.

Finishing the Quilt

Step 1. Prepare template for scallop edge piece. Transfer scallop edge to outer edge of all O pieces. Transfer the twisted-helix quilting design to outer borders. Trace ¼" echo quilting lines around posies center hexagons, beyond outer edges of posies, beyond light green Nine-Patch pieces and beyond inner seam line of O strips.

Step 2. Sandwich thin cotton batting between the completed quilt top and prepared backing piece; pin or baste layers together to hold.

Step 3. Quilt on marked lines or as desired using contrasting quilting threads.

Step 4. When quilting is complete, remove pins or basting. Trim all layers even ¼" beyond the marked scallop line.

Step 5. Prepare 130" of fuchsia bias piping using narrow poly cord. Clip almost to the seam line at inside corners

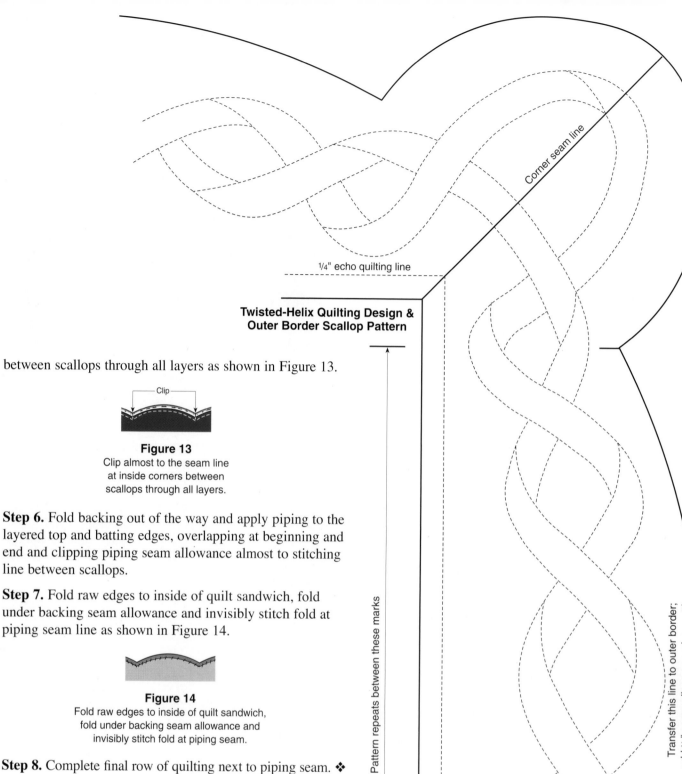

Corner seam line

¼" echo quilting line

**Twisted-Helix Quilting Design &
Outer Border Scallop Pattern**

Pattern repeats between these marks

Transfer this line to outer border;
add ¼" seam allowance when cutting

between scallops through all layers as shown in Figure 13.

Clip

Figure 13
Clip almost to the seam line
at inside corners between
scallops through all layers.

Step 6. Fold backing out of the way and apply piping to the layered top and batting edges, overlapping at beginning and end and clipping piping seam allowance almost to stitching line between scallops.

Step 7. Fold raw edges to inside of quilt sandwich, fold under backing seam allowance and invisibly stitch fold at piping seam line as shown in Figure 14.

Figure 14
Fold raw edges to inside of quilt sandwich,
fold under backing seam allowance and
invisibly stitch fold at piping seam.

Step 8. Complete final row of quilting next to piping seam. ❖

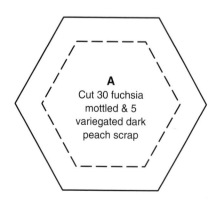

A
Cut 30 fuchsia
mottled & 5
variegated dark
peach scrap

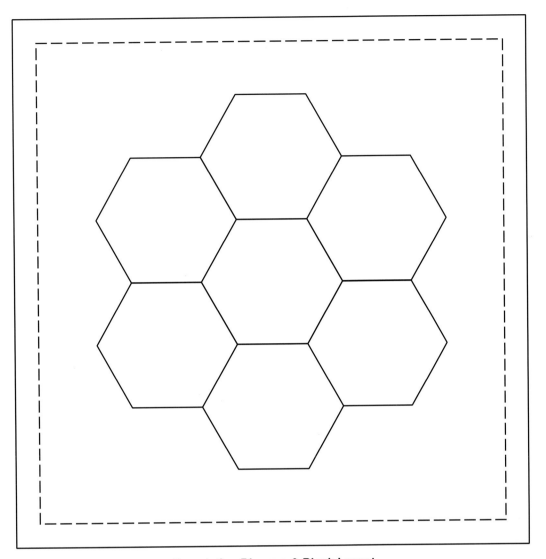

Foundation Diagram & Block Layout

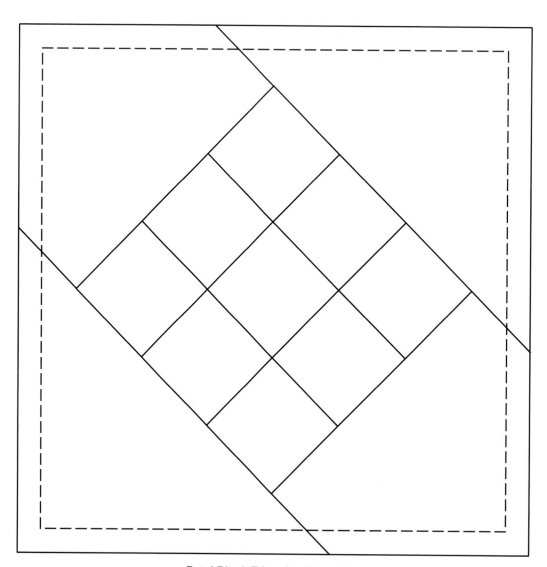

Petal Block Trimming Template

Gifts From an English Garden

Create a floral still-life pillow panel with an entire background design made with ³/8" hexagons.

PROJECT SPECIFICATIONS
Skill Level: Intermediate
Pillow Cover Size: 22" x 16"

MATERIALS
- Scraps of 8 or 9 cream mini prints for background
- Scraps tan scroll print, dark teal mottled, light blue dot, 3 pink and 3 violet prints, white mini print, deep goldenrod solid, green mottled, dark blue mottled, beige print, dark tan mottled, pink stripe and medium teal check
- 1 yard beige plaid
- Thin cotton batting 20" x 17"
- Backing 20" x 17"
- All-purpose thread to match fabrics
- Contrasting quilting thread
- ¹/2 yard 18"-wide plastic-coated freezer paper
- Stapler and staple remover
- Standard paper punch
- Card stock
- 8 (³/4" or ⁷/8") buttons
- 16" pillow form
- Basic sewing tools and supplies, water-erasable marker or pencil, and template material

INSTRUCTIONS

Making Hexagon Background Panel

Step 1. Make two photocopies of the Hexagon Foundations pattern.

Step 2. Prepare template for A using pattern given; cut as directed referring to English Paper Piecing for Hexagons on page 7.

Step 3. Cut five 5" x 7" pieces of freezer paper. Layer each photocopied foundation pattern with two or three pieces of freezer paper; staple through the center of each hexagon.

Step 4. Cut out foundation shapes and remove staples.

Step 5. Iron-fuse foundation shapes on the wrong side of each fabric A piece; fold seam allowances over foundation edges precisely and baste in place.

Step 6. Assemble three blossoms and bowl with stripe referring to Figure 1. Join blossoms and bowl with tan scroll print hexagons between and all around. Fill in with cream hexagons by rows until complete; press.

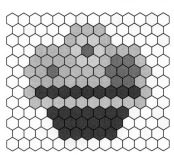

Figure 1
Arrange and join hexagons as shown to create the background.

Step 7. Trim side panel edges straight referring to the Hexagon Panel Layout.

Step 8. Remove basting and paper shapes.

Tip
Shapes that form the straight cut edges of the pieced pillow panel should only have edges prepared that will be stitched to other hexagon edges. For top and bottom panel hexagons, baste four edges only. For side edges, baste three edges only and for corners, baste two edges only.

Making Checker Panel

Step 1. Cut one 1¹/4" x 17" strip each dark tan mottled and beige print. Join strips with right sides together along length; press seam toward darker fabric.

Step 2. Subcut the strip set into thirteen 1¹/4" segments as shown in Figure 2.

1¹/4"

Figure 2
Subcut the strip set into 1¹/4" segments.

Step 3. Join the segments to make a strip as shown in Figure 3; press seams in one direction.

Figure 3
Join the segments to make a strip.

Step 4. Center and sew the pieced strip to the bottom edges of the hexagon panel as shown in Figure 4; press seams toward strip. Trim excess strip even with panel.

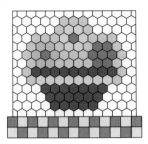

Figure 4
Center and sew the pieced strip to the bottom edges of the hexagon panel.

Step 5. Measure and trim completed pieced panel to 9¹/₂" x 9¹/₂".

Appliqué Details

Step 1. Prepare templates for daisy petal and frond shapes using patterns given; cut as directed on each shape, adding a ¹/₈"–¹/₄" seam allowance all around when cutting.

Step 2. Fold seam allowance edges of each shape to the wrong side along marked seam line and baste to hold.

Gifts From an English Garden
Placement Diagram
22" x 16"

Step 3. Transfer the Appliqué Layout Diagram to the pieced background using a water-erasable marker or pencil.

Step 4. Position basted appliqué shapes on the marked areas in numerical order referring to the Appliqué Layout Diagram; appliqué in place.

Step 5. Prepare daisy centers and frond circles by cutting circle patches from goldenrod and dark blue scraps. Cut daisy center circle and punch (using standard paper punch) frond circle forms from card stock.

Step 6. Hand-baste a line of stitching within seam allowance of a circle with matching thread, leaving needle attached. Place a card-stock circle form on the wrong side of the basted circle within the basted line as shown in Figure 5; pull thread to gather fabric around circle form, again referring to Figure 5. Backstitch to secure; repeat for all circles.

Figure 5
Place a card-stock circle form on the wrong side of the basted circle within the basted line; pull thread to gather fabric around circle form.

Step 7. Position and appliqué circles in place with the attached thread.

Adding Borders

Step 1. Cut two 1" x 9¹/₂" B strips and two 1" x 10¹/₂" C strips pink stripe. Sew B to opposite sides and C to the top and bottom of the pieced panel; press seams toward strips.

Step 2. Cut two 1¼" x 10½" D and two 1¼" x 12" E strips beige print. Sew D to opposite sides and E to the top and bottom of the pieced panel; press seams toward strips.

Step 3. Cut two 1¾" x 12" F and two 1¾" x 14½" G strips medium teal check. Sew F to opposite sides and G to the top and bottom of the pieced panel; press seams toward strips.

Step 4. Cut two 1½" x 14½" H and two 8¼" x 16½" I strips beige plaid. Sew H to the top and bottom and I to opposite sides of the pieced panel; press seams toward strips.

Finishing the Pillow

Step 1. Transfer quilting lines to panel referring to Figure 6.

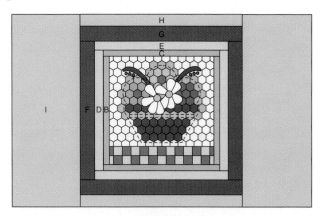

Figure 6
Transfer quilting lines to panel.

Step 2. Sandwich thin cotton batting between the completed quilt top and prepared backing piece behind center panel area as shown in Figure 7; pin or baste layers together to hold.

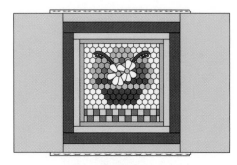

Figure 7
Layer batting and backing under center panel as shown.

Step 3. Quilt on marked lines and in the ditch of border seams and appliqué edges using contrasting quilting thread.

Step 4. When quilting is complete, remove pins or basting. Trim batting and backing edges even with top and bottom edges and 2½" beyond quilting at panel sides. *Note: Side edges of batting and backing should extend*

¼"–⅜" under inner fold edge of hem when folded in place to be caught in hem topstitching.

Step 5. Cut a J pillow back panel 30" x 16½" from beige plaid. Sew to front panel along upper edge; press seam toward J.

Step 6. Press a double 2" hem along panel side edges as shown in Figure 8. Unfold hems and stitch lower edges of front and back panels; press seams toward J. *Note: The J back panel should match the pieced front panel exactly. Compare the two and trim J to match pieced front.*

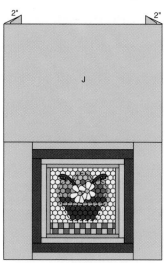

Figure 8
Press a 2" double hem along side edges.

Step 7. Overcast raw edges of seams; refold double hem and topstitch with matching thread next to hem fold from inside.

Step 8. Mark buttonhole positions on front hemmed area referring to Figure 9. Stitch 1" buttonholes and cut open. Position and stitch buttons below buttonholes. Insert pillow form and fasten buttons. *Note: If pillow form will remain inside cover permanently, buttonholes may be eliminated and buttons stitched in place through all layers.* ❖

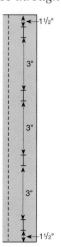

Figure 9
Mark buttonhole position on front hemmed area.

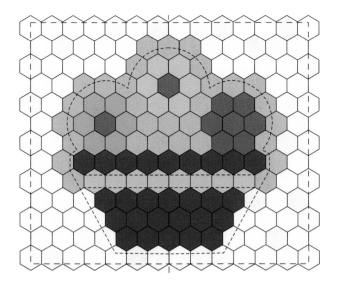

Hexagon Panel Layout
Outer dashed lines indicate seam line (trim ¼" beyond);
inner dashed lines indicate quilting design lines.

A
Cut 1 each violet print, 6 each pink print,
8 light blue dot, 27 dark teal mottled, 30
tan scroll print & 90 cream mini prints

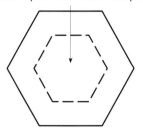

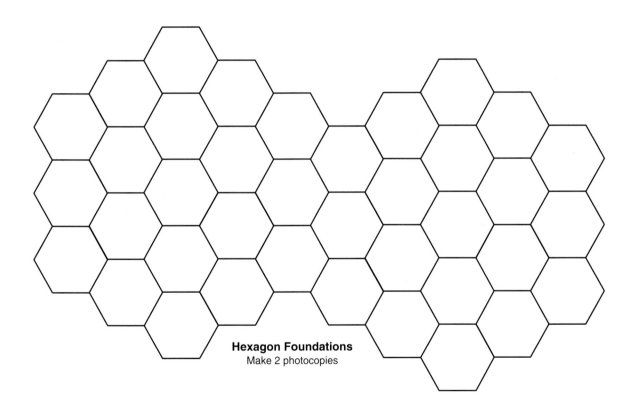

Hexagon Foundations
Make 2 photocopies

Frond
Cut 2 green mottled
(reverse 1)

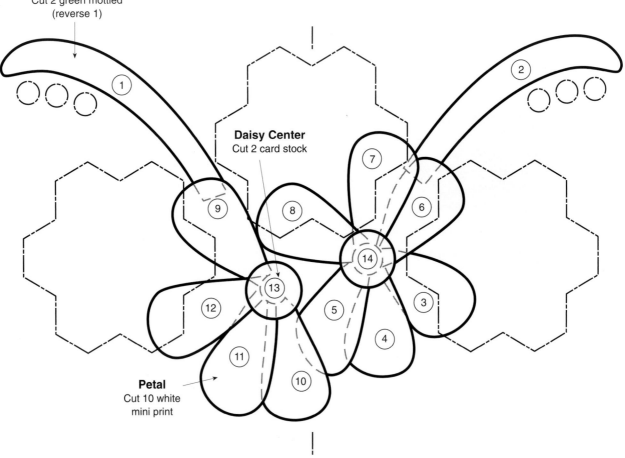

Daisy Center
Cut 2 card stock

Petal
Cut 10 white
mini print

Appliqué Layout Diagram

Large Circle
Cut 2
goldenrod solid

Small Circle
Cut 6 dark
blue mottled

Patchwork Pieced Hexagons

A precisely pieced background is beneath the appliquéd motifs in the Twelve Days of Christmas Wall Quilt. It is made up of a variety of pieced hexagon styles in a variety of fabrics.

1

EQUAL-HALF PIECED PATCHES

1A. Hexagons for English paper-foundation patchwork can be made up of more than one fabric for added interest. For the equal-half pieced hexagons, cut and machine-stitch two beige patches $2\frac{1}{2}$" x $4\frac{3}{4}$"; press seam open.

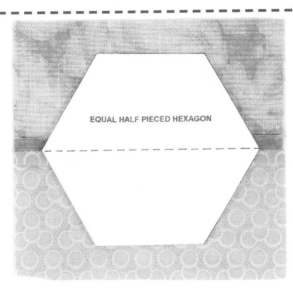

1B. Position a trimmed paper hexagon with equal-half dividing guideline over backside of prepared fabric patch, aligning dashed line exactly over seam. Secure in place with fabric glue stick.

1C. Trim excess fabric $\frac{1}{4}$" beyond paper shape edges. Fold and baste seam allowance over edge of paper. Align and whipstitch folded edges of prepared shapes.

2

SINGLE-RIDGE PATCHES

2A. For single-ridge pieced hexagons, cut and join one beige patch $3\frac{1}{2}$" x 4" and one cream or beige patch $1\frac{3}{4}$" x 4". Press seams toward narrower patch. Some of the single-ridge patches are part of the multitone background. For these, use any two beige scraps. For those that create star points, the narrow patch should be cream.

Tip

To reduce bulk of seam allowance in folded edge, try joining patches with shortened machine-stitch length (for seam security), then trim seam allowance to $\frac{1}{8}$" after it is pressed to one side.

SINGLE RIDGE PIECED HEXAGON
&
PARTIAL PLAIN HEXAGON

2B. Position a trimmed single-ridge paper hexagon with dividing guideline exactly over seam. Secure in place with fabric glue stick.

SINGLE RIDGE PIECED HEXAGON
&
PARTIAL PLAIN HEXAGON

2C. Trim excess fabric $\frac{1}{4}$" beyond paper shape; fold and baste seam allowance back.

3

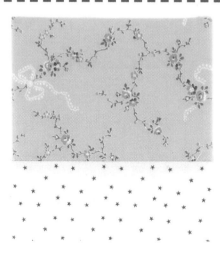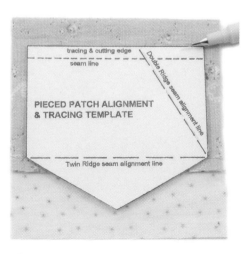

tracing & cutting edge
seam line
Double Ridge seam alignment line

PIECED PATCH ALIGNMENT
& TRACING TEMPLATE

Twin Ridge seam alignment line

TWIN-RIDGE PATCHES

3A. For twin-ridge pieced hexagons, cut and join one beige patch 3" x 4" and one cream patch $1\frac{3}{4}$" x 4". Center tracing template H on backside of patch with twin-ridge guideline aligned at seam and mark cutting-line edge.

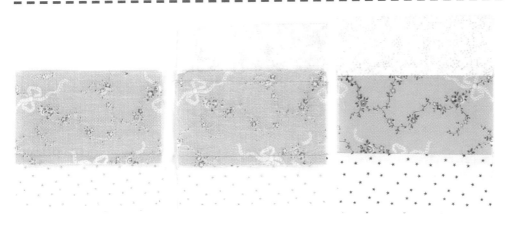

3B. Rotary-trim on marked cutting line. Cut and join a second 1³/₄" x 4" cream patch along cut edge; press toward cream strip.

3C. Position a trimmed twin-ridge paper hexagon with dividing guideline exactly over seam; secure in place with fabric glue stick.

TWIN RIDGE PIECED HEXAGON

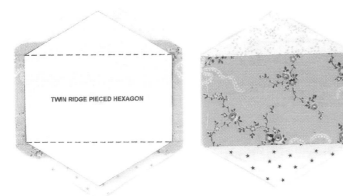

3D. Trim excess fabric ¹/₄" beyond paper shape; fold and baste seam allowance back.

TWIN RIDGE PIECED HEXAGON

DOUBLE-RIDGE PATCHES

4A. For double-ridge pieced hexagons, cut and join one beige patch 3³/₄" x 4¹/₂" and one cream patch 1³/₄" x 4¹/₂". Press seams toward narrower patch. Center tracing template H on the backside of the patch with double-ridge guideline aligned at seam; mark cutting-line edge.

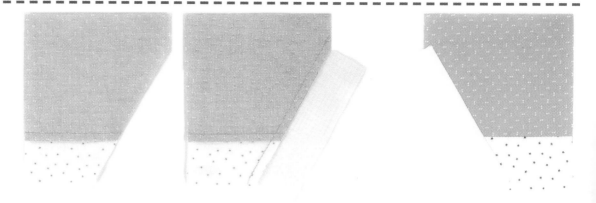

4B. Rotary-trim on marked cutting line. Cut and join 1³/₄" x 4¹/₂" cream strip along cut edge; press toward the just-added cream strip.

4C. Position a trimmed double-ridge paper hexagon with dividing guidelines exactly over seams; secure in place with fabric glue stick.

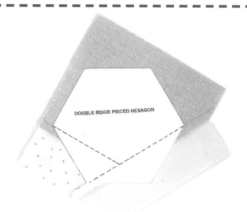

4D. Trim excess fabric ¹/₄" beyond paper shape; fold and baste seam allowance back.

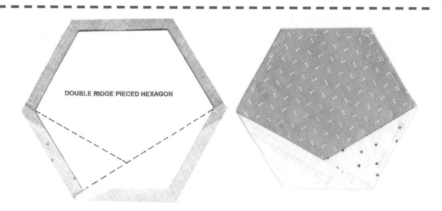

Twelve Days of Christmas

The full dozen characters from the Twelve Days of Christmas *song are featured in hand-appliquéd detail on a multitoned background of paper-pieced hexagons.*

PROJECT SPECIFICATIONS

Skill Level: Advanced

Quilt Size: Approximately 43" x 52½"

MATERIALS

- Scraps of a variety of prints, solids and stripes for appliqué (see appliqué patterns for color suggestions)
- Scraps of 10–12 light-to-medium beige mini prints for pieced backgrounds
- ⅛ yard each 6–8 cream mini prints for twisting stars
- ½ yard dark green print for Celtic appliqué
- ¾ yard green ½"-wide stripe for borders
- ⅞ yard red pin dot for corners, borders and ribbon appliqué
- 1 yard black tone-on-tone for borders and binding
- 1 yard beige solid for appliqué background
- Thin cotton batting 49" x 59"
- Backing 49" x 59"
- Neutral color all-purpose thread
- Contrasting quilting thread
- Color pencils
- Goldenrod, deep red, black, light and medium blue, medium and dark green, brown and beige 6-strand embroidery floss
- Basic sewing tools and supplies, card stock, ¼" hole punch, template material, tape, fabric glue stick and water-erasable marker or pencil

PROJECT NOTES

Pieced hexagon units frame the center background appliqué area. The hexagon units are pieced using light-to-medium beige prints with cream mini prints for star points. Refer to Patchwork Pieced Hexagons on page 85 for step-by-step instructions for making each type of pieced hexagon.

Appliqué patterns are given full size with color suggestions and stitch detail suggestions. Appliqué pieces within motifs in numerical order as marked on patterns.

Patterns for small circle appliqués may be made of card stock with a ¼" hole punch. Cut fabric ⅛" larger than punch-dot circle all around. Stitch a basting stitch all around, place card-stock circle in center on wrong side of fabric and gather fabric around circle (see pages 81 and 84).

INSTRUCTIONS

Center Panel Background Patchwork Preparation

Step 1. Prepare a 31½" x 41" rectangle beige solid for background. Fold in quarters and crease to mark the center.

Step 2. Prepare 18 copies of the hexagon foundation diagram on page 109 and six G pieces. Cut out pattern shapes on traced lines to make paper foundations for each type of hexagon. Discard unneeded paper pieces. Prepare template for H.

Step 3. Create pieced hexagon units referring to Patchwork Pieced Hexagons on page 85 for step-by-step instructions and referring to Figure 1. *Note: The small pieced sections of some D and all E and F hexagons that create the star points are cut from cream mini prints.* Cut fabric patches as directed in Figure 1 for size and color.

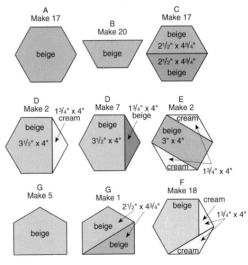

Figure 1
Create pieced hexagon units as shown.

Step 4. Join A, B and D pieces as shown in Figure 2 to make Section 1 for bottom edge; join pieces referring to English Paper Piecing for Hexagons on page 7. *Note: Corner B pieces will be trimmed later.*

Step 5. Join B, C, F and G pieces as shown in Figure 3 for Section 2 and Section 2R. *Note: F and C pieces will be trimmed later.*

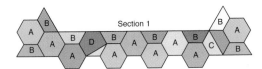

Figure 2
Join A, B and D pieces to make Section 1 for bottom edge.

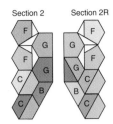

Figure 3
Join B, C, F and G pieces for
Section 2 and Section 2R.

Step 6. Join A, B, C, D, F and G pieces as shown in Figure 4 for Section 3 and Section 3R. *Note: A and C pieces will be trimmed later.*

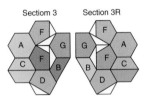

Figure 4
Join A, B, C, D, F and G pieces
for Section 3 and Section 3R.

Step 7. Join A, B, C, D, E and F pieces as shown in Figure 5 for Section 4 and Section 4R. *Note: A, B, C, D and F pieces will be trimmed later.*

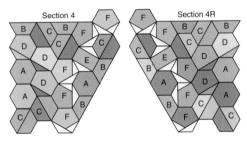

Figure 5
Join A, B, C, D, E and F pieces
for Section 4 and Section 4R.

Step 8. Arrange pieced sections on the 31½" x 41" beige solid background rectangle, centering A on Section 1 at bottom edge and centering a single A between Sections 4 and 4R at top edge and centering the seam of Sections 3 and 3R C pieces on side edges referring to Figure 6. Join sections.

Step 9. Trim excess on all outside edges even with background rectangle as shown in Figure 7. *Note: This pieced section should be 31½" x 41" at this point for borders to fit later.*

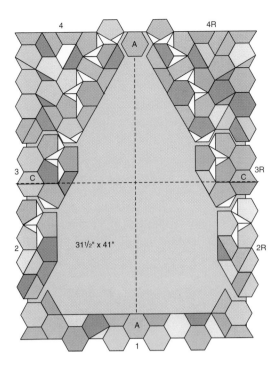

Figure 6
Arrange pieced sections on the 31½" x 41" beige solid background rectangle, centering A on Section 1 at bottom edge and centering a single A between Sections 4 and 4R at top edge and centering the seam of Sections 3 and 3R C pieces on side edges.

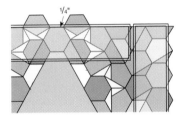

Figure 7
Trim excess on all outside edges
even with background rectangle.

Adding Borders

Step 1. Prepare templates for border pieces L–T using full-size patterns given; cut as directed on each piece, adding a ¼" seam allowance around each piece. Stay-stitch along bias edges of the L and M triangles to prevent stretching.

Step 2. Join three L and four LR triangles to make a side strip as shown in Figure 8; press seams in one direction. Repeat for two side border strips.

Figure 8
Join L and LR triangles to make border
strips as shown; add M and MR to ends.

Step 3. Join three L and two LR triangles to make a top strip, again referring to Figure 8; press seams in one direction. Repeat for bottom strip.

Step 4. Sew M and MR triangles to ends of each side and top and bottom strip, again referring to Figure 8, stopping seams on the inside edge at the seam line of M and MR; press seams away from M pieces.

Step 5. Cut four 1¹/₂" x 38" J strips red pin dot; center and sew a strip to each long side of each side border strip; press seams toward strips.

Step 6. Using a rotary cutter and ruler, trim excess strip continuing the angle of the L and M triangles on the strip as shown in Figure 9.

Figure 9
Trim excess strip continuing the angle of
the L and M triangles on the strip.

Step 7. Cut four 1¹/₂" x 28" K strips red pin dot; center and sew a strip to each long side of the top and bottom border strips; press seams toward strips.

Step 8. Use a rotary ruler and cutter to trim excess strips as in Step 6 and referring to Figure 9.

Step 9. To make border corners, sew O, Q, QR and P to N to complete an N unit, stitching mitered seams at intersections of pieces referring to Figure 10; press seams away from N. Repeat sewing Q, QR, S and T to R to complete an R unit, again referring to Figure 10. Repeat for two and two reversed of each unit.

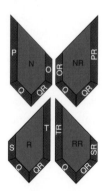

Figure 10
Join pieces to make
N, NR, R and RR
units as shown.

Step 10. Set in an N and NR unit on opposite ends of each side border strip as shown in Figure 11; press seams toward the N units. Repeat with R and RR units on opposite ends of the top and bottom border strips, again referring to Figure 11.

Figure 11
Sew N and NR units to each side border strip; repeat
with R and RR units on top and bottom border strips.

Step 11. Sew the side border strips to opposite sides and the top and bottom strips to the quilt center; press seams toward strips.

Appliqué Details

Step 1. Prepare full-size patterns for each appliqué motif and cut out referring to color suggestions given on each pattern piece, adding a seam allowance all around for hand appliqué.

Step 2. Stitch the complete design before applying to background as directed on each motif.

Step 3. Arrange prepared tree motifs on the pieced top in numerical order referring to Figures 12 and 13 and the Placement Diagram for positioning of motifs on the center background area; hand-stitch in place.

Figure 12
Arrange leaves and trunk on a flat
surface as shown; add pear clusters.

Figure 13
Arrange prepared tree motifs on center
background in numerical order as shown.

Step 4. Arrange remaining motifs around the tree referring to the Placement Diagram for positioning.

Step 5. Add embroidered details referring to suggestions given with each motif. *Note: Black small dashed lines are quilting lines.*

Step 6. Prepare 162" of ¹/₄"-wide finished dark green print bias. *Note: To prepare bias, cut strips ³/₄" wide; fold with wrong sides together and stitch a ¹/₈" seam. Press with seam centered on the back to make finished bias strips for Celtic heart.* Position and baste in place at guidelines, shaping around curves, overlapping at intersections and creating mitered folds at square corners as shown on N and R pattern pieces. Trim excess at strip ends and overlap ends. Appliqué exposed folded edges.

Finishing the Quilt

Step 1. Transfer quilting design lines to corner panels. Transfer quilting lines to all appliqué motifs as marked on patterns. Sketch tree cascading lines on exposed background appliqué center panel and starburst lines radiating from star points in the pieced background.

Step 2. Sandwich thin cotton batting between the completed quilt top and prepared backing piece; pin or baste layers together to hold.

Step 3. Quilt on marked lines and in the ditch around appliqué figures and elements and within as desired. Echo-

Twelve Days of Christmas
Placement Diagram
Approximately 43" x 52¹/₂"

quilt ¹/₄" beyond entire appliquéd section, next to seams of hexagon patchwork and in borders following regular intervals of stripes in border triangles. When quilting is complete, remove pins or basting.

Step 4. Prepare a 5³/₄-yard length of 2¹/₄"-wide bias binding from black tone-on-tone and apply to edges to finish. ❖

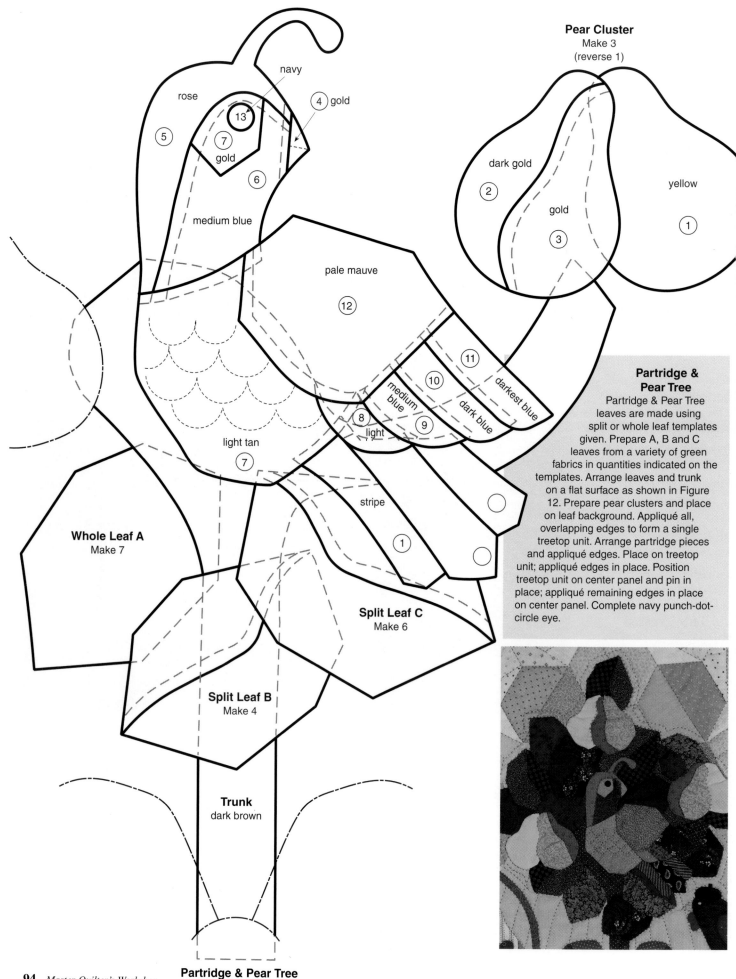

Pear Cluster
Make 3
(reverse 1)

navy

rose

⑤

⑬

④ gold

⑦

gold

⑥

medium blue

dark gold

②

gold

③

yellow

①

pale mauve

⑫

⑪

medium blue

⑩

darkest blue

⑧

light

⑨

dark blue

light tan

⑦

stripe

①

Whole Leaf A
Make 7

Split Leaf C
Make 6

Split Leaf B
Make 4

Trunk
dark brown

Partridge & Pear Tree
Partridge & Pear Tree leaves are made using split or whole leaf templates given. Prepare A, B and C leaves from a variety of green fabrics in quantities indicated on the templates. Arrange leaves and trunk on a flat surface as shown in Figure 12. Prepare pear clusters and place on leaf background. Appliqué all, overlapping edges to form a single treetop unit. Arrange partridge pieces and appliqué edges. Place on treetop unit; appliqué edges in place. Position treetop unit on center panel and pin in place; appliqué remaining edges in place on center panel. Complete navy punch-dot-circle eye.

Partridge & Pear Tree

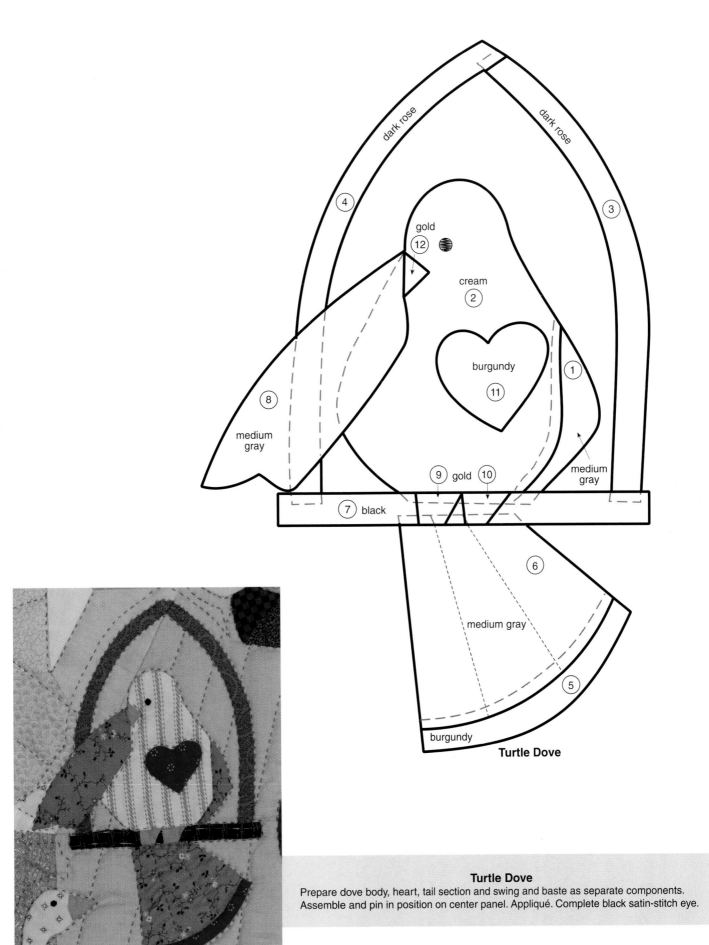

dark rose

dark rose

④

③

gold

⑫

cream

②

burgundy

⑪

①

⑧

medium
gray

⑨ gold ⑩

medium
gray

⑦ black

⑥

⑤

medium gray

burgundy

Turtle Dove

Turtle Dove
Prepare dove body, heart, tail section and swing and baste as separate components.
Assemble and pin in position on center panel. Appliqué. Complete black satin-stitch eye.

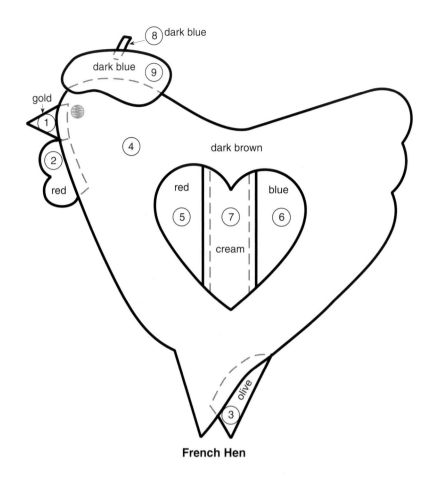

French Hen

French Hen

Prepare as complete component. Position on center panel and stitch in place, inserting dark blue narrowly rolled short strip under hat for tab. Complete goldenrod satin-stitch eye.

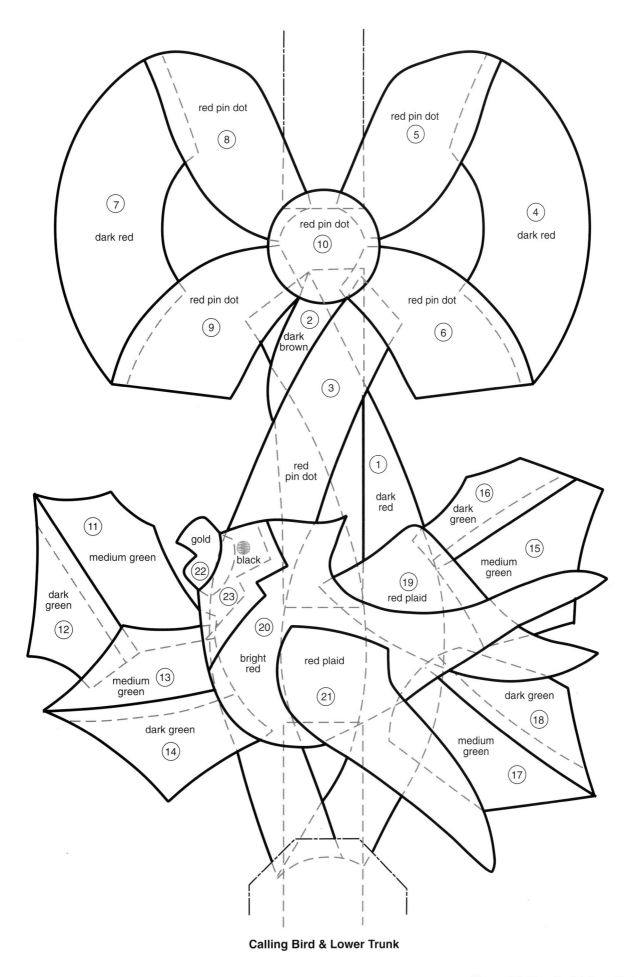

Calling Bird & Lower Trunk

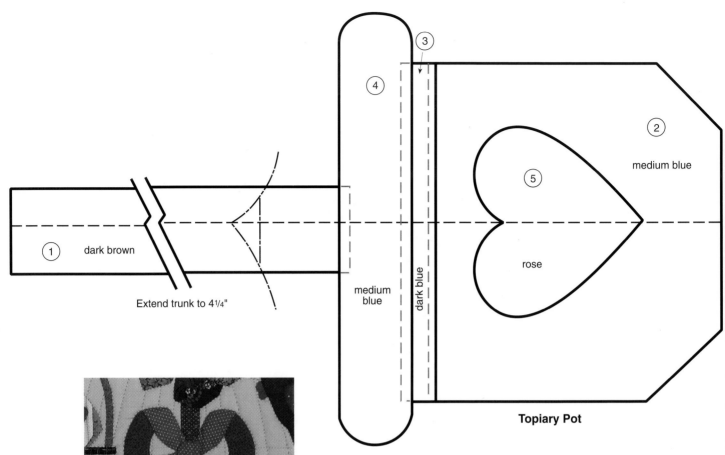

① dark brown

Extend trunk to 4¼"

④ medium blue

③

② medium blue

dark blue

⑤ rose

Topiary Pot

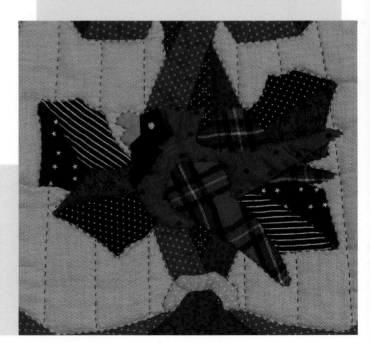

Calling Bird & Lower Trunk
Prepare holly leaves, bird, lower ribbon sections, then assemble as complete component. Position on center panel and stitch in place. Complete beige satin-stitch eye.

Bow, Ribbons & Upper Trunk
Prepare bow sections as a unit. Position with trunk and crisscross ribbon sections on center panel and stitch in place.

Topiary Pot
Prepare pot patch by joining a 1" x 4½" strip of dark blue fabric for rim shadow to a 4½" x 3½" medium blue for pot bottom. Press seams toward dark strip. Use pot template to align shadow guideline with patch seam; trace and trim top rim. Complete heart appliqué, then position pot and trunk on center panel and stitch in place.

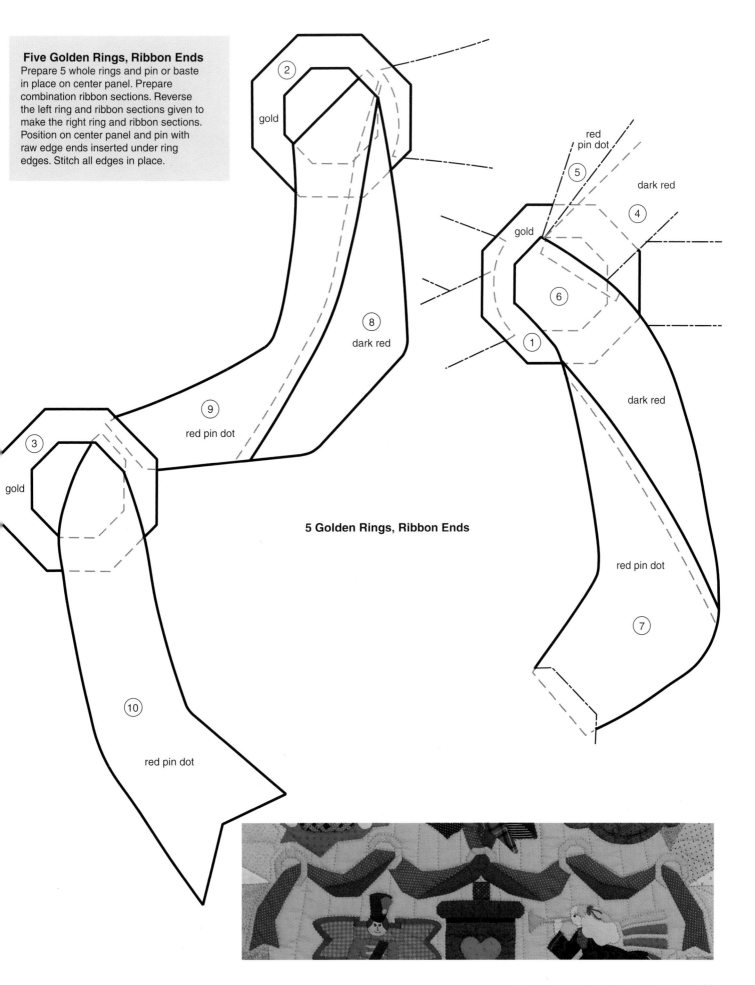

Five Golden Rings, Ribbon Ends
Prepare 5 whole rings and pin or baste in place on center panel. Prepare combination ribbon sections. Reverse the left ring and ribbon sections given to make the right ring and ribbon sections. Position on center panel and pin with raw edge ends inserted under ring edges. Stitch all edges in place.

② gold

⑧ dark red

⑨ red pin dot

③ gold

⑩ red pin dot

red pin dot

⑤

dark red

④

gold

⑥

①

dark red

red pin dot

⑦

5 Golden Rings, Ribbon Ends

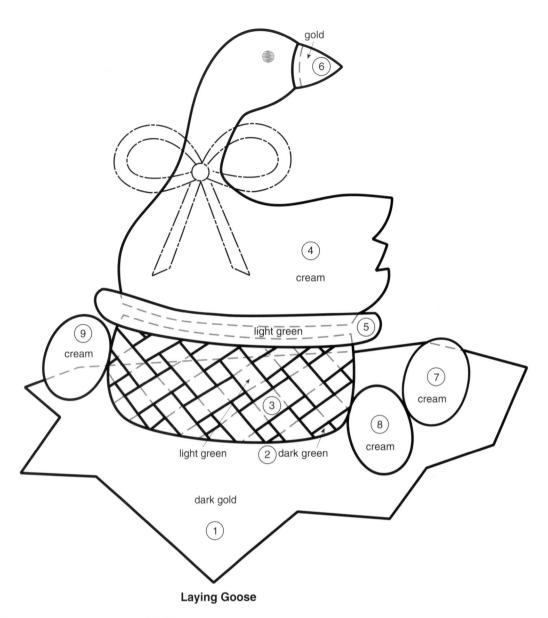

gold

6

4
cream

9
cream

light green 5

3

light green   2 dark green

7
cream

8
cream

dark gold

1

Laying Goose

Laying Goose

Prepare hay, eggs and goose separately. Prepare dimensional basket with dark green base shape and prepared ¼"-wide light green bias tubes woven over top. Edges of all layers are turned under and basted. Prepare rim and stitch in place. Assemble all components as a complete unit, then position on center panel and stitch in place. For ribbon and bow, prepare 12"-long, ⅛"-wide medium blue bias tube. Stitch in place in center of goose neck. Finish ends of remaining piece, then tie in bow and tack in place. Complete medium blue satin-stitch eye.

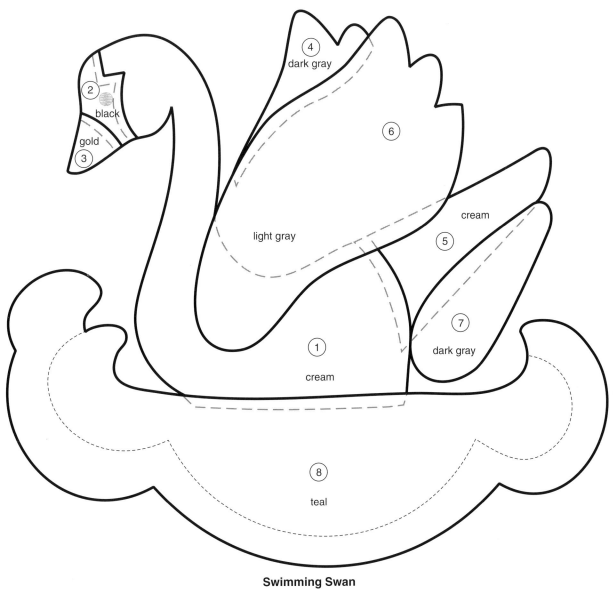

Swimming Swan

Swimming Swan
Prepare swan and water as complete component. Position on center panel and stitch in place. Complete goldenrod satin-stitch eye.

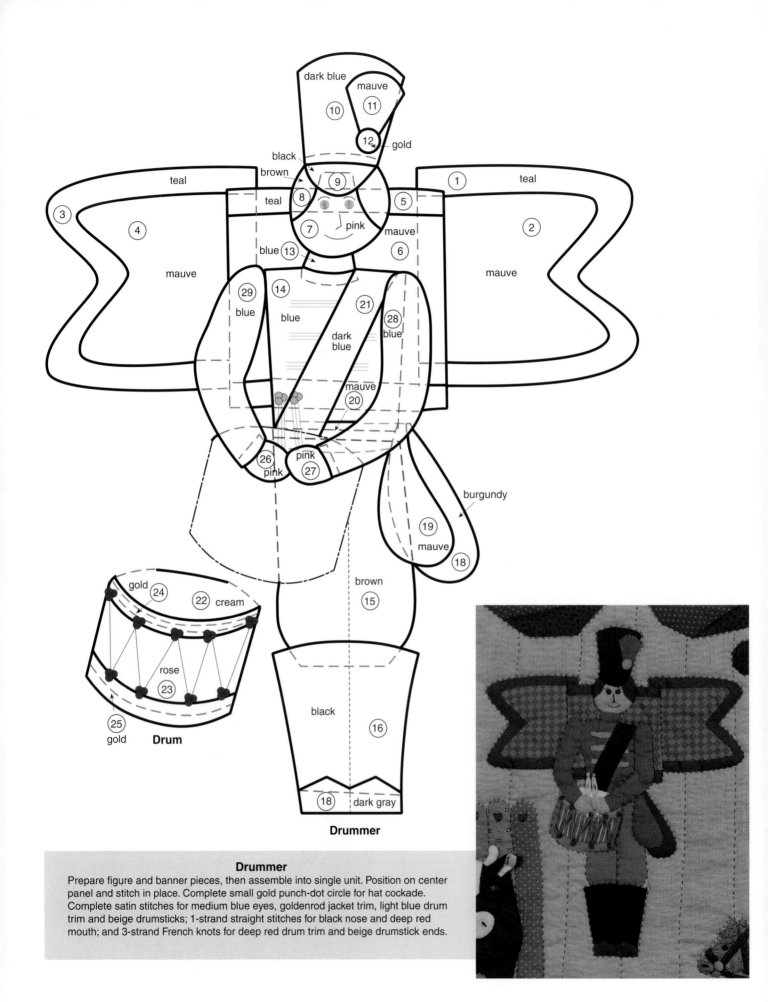

dark blue

mauve

10

11

12 — gold

black

brown

teal

9

teal

8

teal

1

teal

3

4

5

2

mauve

mauve

mauve

7

pink

6

mauve

blue 13

blue

29

14

21

blue

blue

blue

28

blue

dark
blue

mauve

20

mauve

19

burgundy

18

mauve

26

pink

pink

27

gold 24

22 cream

brown

15

rose

23

25

gold

Drum

black

16

18 dark gray

Drummer

Drummer

Prepare figure and banner pieces, then assemble into single unit. Position on center panel and stitch in place. Complete small gold punch-dot circle for hat cockade. Complete satin stitches for medium blue eyes, goldenrod jacket trim, light blue drum trim and beige drumsticks; 1-strand straight stitches for black nose and deep red mouth; and 3-strand French knots for deep red drum trim and beige drumstick ends.

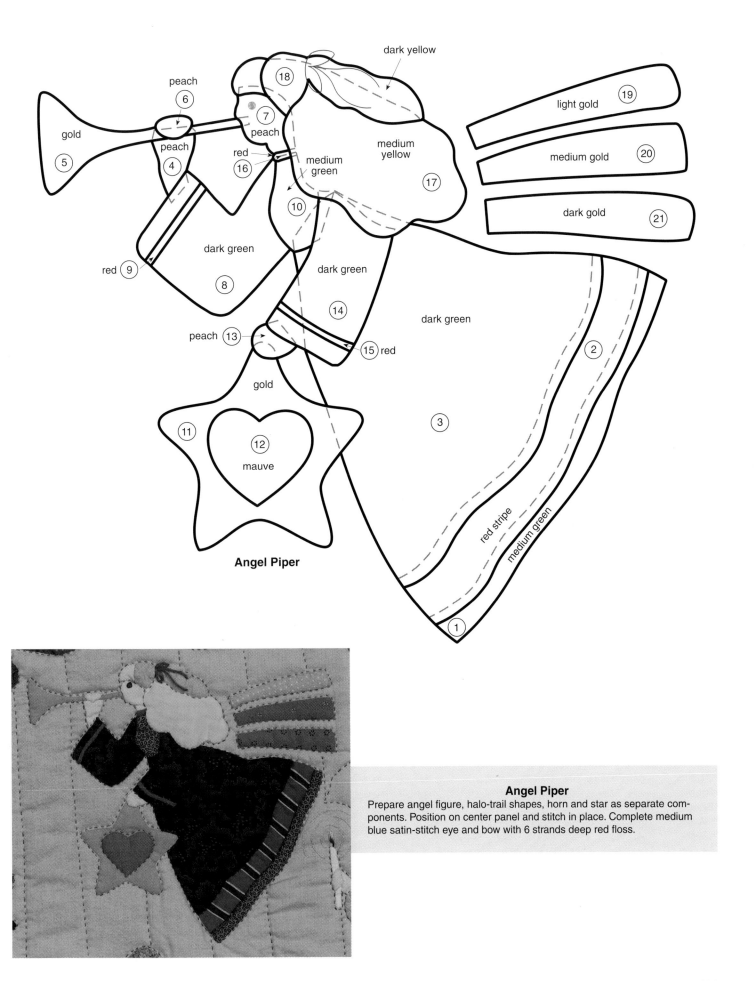

peach
⑥

gold
⑤

peach
④

peach
⑦

peach

red
⑯

⑱

dark yellow

medium
green

medium
yellow

⑩

⑰

light gold
⑲

medium gold
⑳

dark gold
㉑

dark green
⑧

red ⑨

dark green

⑭

dark green

peach ⑬

⑮ red

gold

⑪

⑫

mauve

②

③

Angel Piper

red stripe

medium green

①

Angel Piper
Prepare angel figure, halo-trail shapes, horn and star as separate components. Position on center panel and stitch in place. Complete medium blue satin-stitch eye and bow with 6 strands deep red floss.

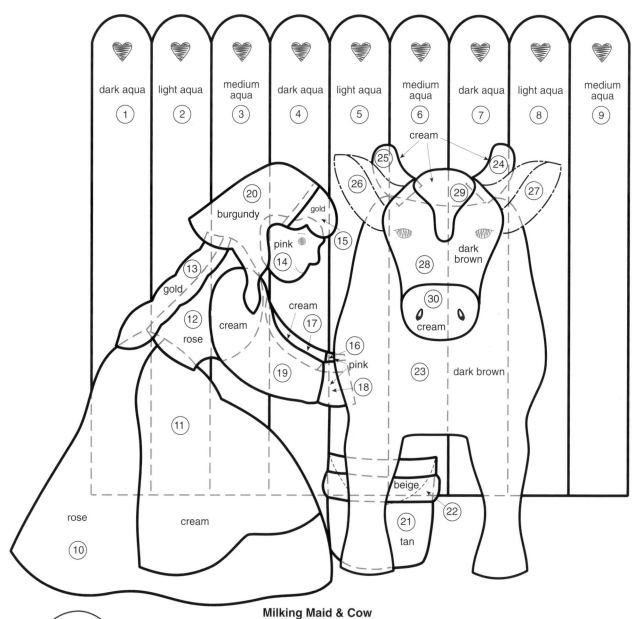

dark aqua (1)
light aqua (2)
medium aqua (3)
dark aqua (4)
light aqua (5)
medium aqua (6)
dark aqua (7)
light aqua (8)
medium aqua (9)

(20) burgundy
gold
pink (14)
(15)
(13) gold
(12) rose
cream
cream (17)
(19)
(16) pink
(18)
(11)
rose
cream
(10)

cream
(25) (24)
(26) (29) (27)
dark brown
(28)
(30) cream
(23) dark brown
beige (22)
(21) tan

Milking Maid & Cow

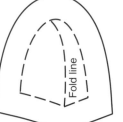

Fold line

Dimensional Ear Template
Cut 2 each cream & dark brown
(reverse 1 of each)

Milking Maid & Cow

Prepare 9 fence pickets from varied aqua fabrics, then position and stitch in place. Prepare maid, bucket and cow as complete components. Prepare dimensional ears: prepare separate inner cream and outer dark brown shapes with curved edges turned under, then layer with seam allowances enclosed. Whipstitch edges. Fold upper edge of ear down on dashed line. Position components over fence and center panel, inserting ear raw edge ends under cow head. Complete satin stitches for medium blue maid's eye, beige cow's eyes and deep red hearts on fence; 1-strand straight stitch for deep red maid's mouth and brown maid's eyebrow; brown lazy-daisy cow's nostrils; and 3-strand chain stitches for black bucket handle.

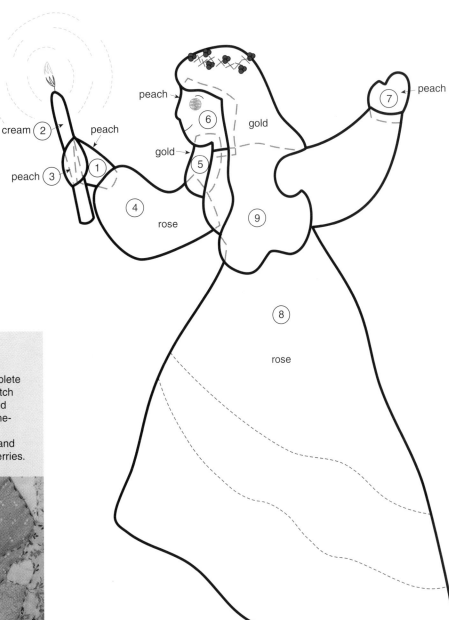

cream ② peach

peach ①

peach ③

4 rose

peach

gold

6

gold ⑤

⑦ peach

9

8

rose

Dancing Lady

Dancing Lady

Prepare complete figure as a single component.
Position on center panel and stitch in place. Complete
medium blue satin-stitch eye, 1-strand straight-stitch
black wick, deep red and goldenrod lazy-daisy and
straight-stitch flame and goldenrod 1-strand outline-
stitch candlelight halo. Create head wreath with
overlapping 2-strand straight stitches in medium and
dark green with 1 strand deep red French-knot berries.

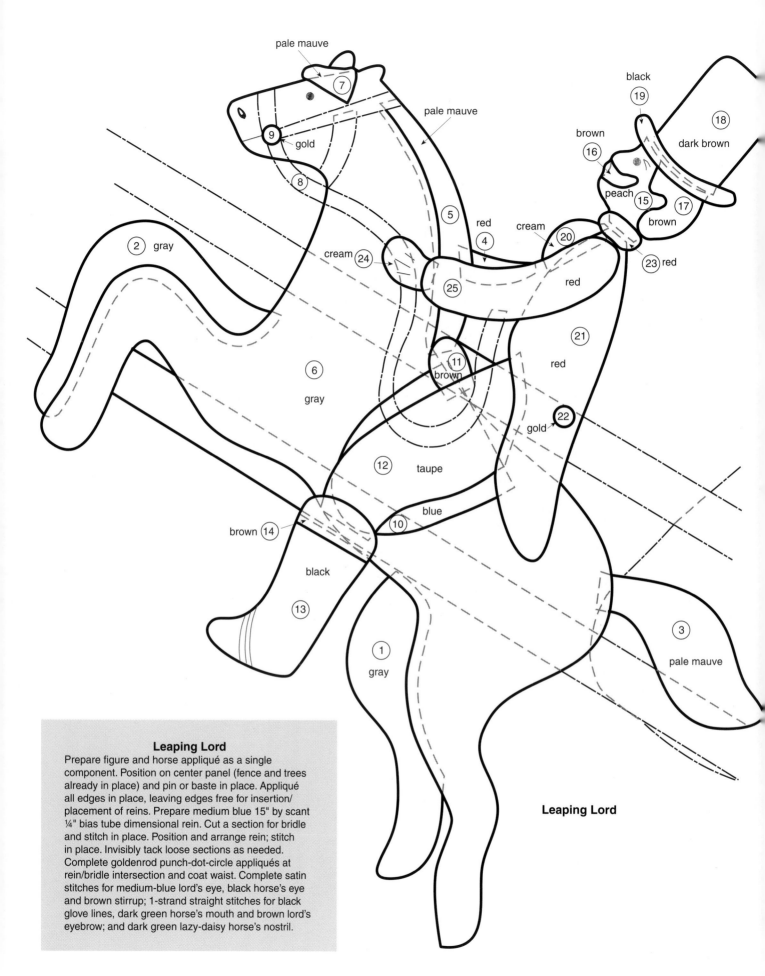

pale mauve

7

pale mauve

black
19

brown
16

peach
15

brown

dark brown
18

brown
17

gold
9

8

5

red
4

cream

cream
24

20

25

red

red

21

red

6

gray

11
brown

2 gray

23 red

22
gold

12 taupe

blue

10

brown 14

black

13

1
gray

3

pale mauve

Leaping Lord
Prepare figure and horse appliqué as a single
component. Position on center panel (fence and trees
already in place) and pin or baste in place. Appliqué
all edges in place, leaving edges free for insertion/
placement of reins. Prepare medium blue 15" by scant
¼" bias tube dimensional rein. Cut a section for bridle
and stitch in place. Position and arrange rein; stitch
in place. Invisibly tack loose sections as needed.
Complete goldenrod punch-dot-circle appliqués at
rein/bridle intersection and coat waist. Complete satin
stitches for medium-blue lord's eye, black horse's eye
and brown stirrup; 1-strand straight stitches for black
glove lines, dark green horse's mouth and brown lord's
eyebrow; and dark green lazy-daisy horse's nostril.

Leaping Lord

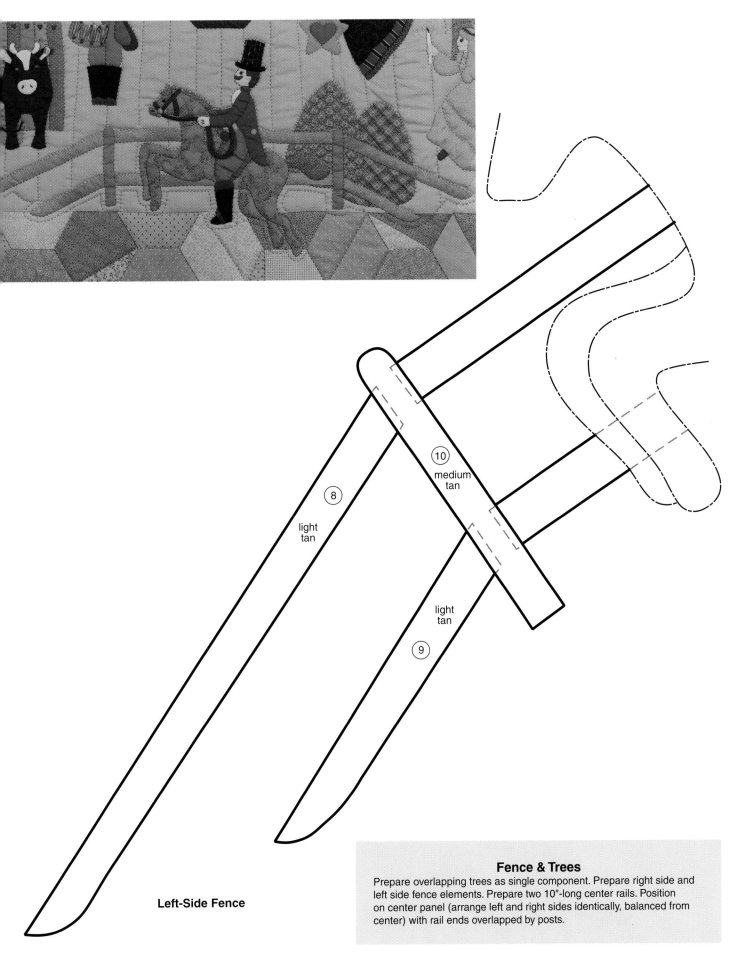

(8) light tan

(10) medium tan

(9) light tan

Left-Side Fence

Fence & Trees
Prepare overlapping trees as single component. Prepare right side and left side fence elements. Prepare two 10"-long center rails. Position on center panel (arrange left and right sides identically, balanced from center) with rail ends overlapped by posts.

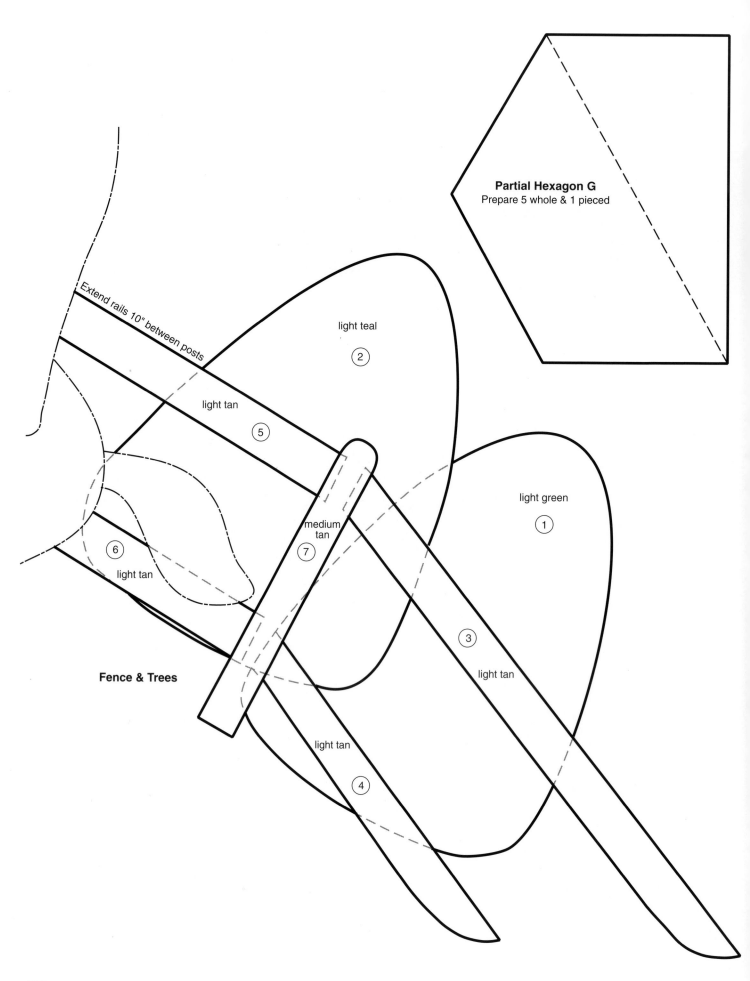

Partial Hexagon G
Prepare 5 whole & 1 pieced

Extend rails 10" between posts

light teal
②

light tan
⑤

light green
①

medium tan
⑦

light tan
⑥

light tan
③

Fence & Trees

light tan
④

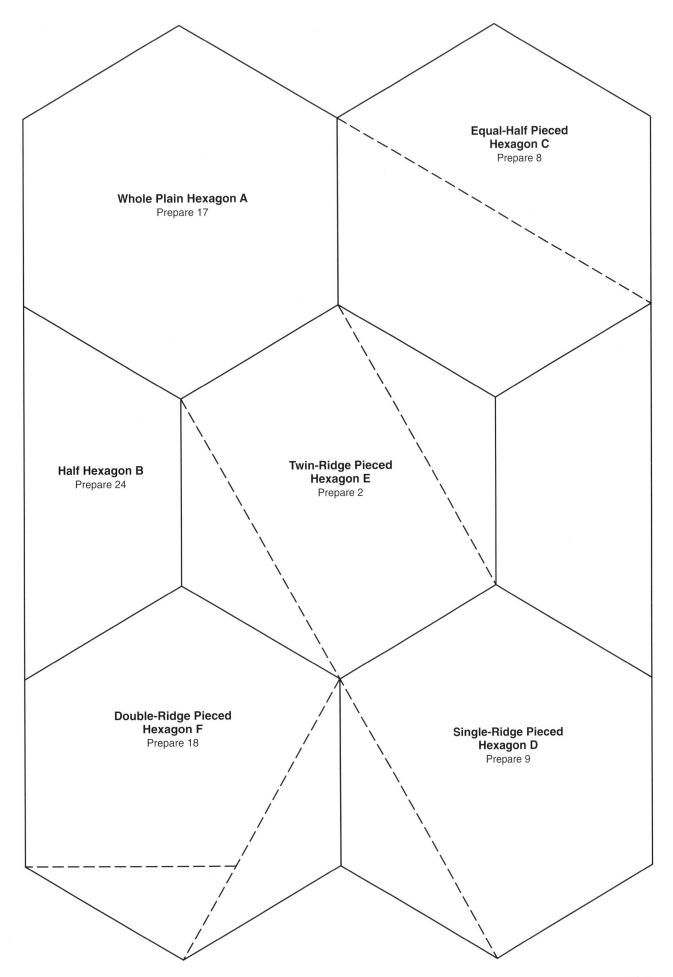

Whole Plain Hexagon A
Prepare 17

Equal-Half Pieced Hexagon C
Prepare 8

Half Hexagon B
Prepare 24

Twin-Ridge Pieced Hexagon E
Prepare 2

Double-Ridge Pieced Hexagon F
Prepare 18

Single-Ridge Pieced Hexagon D
Prepare 9

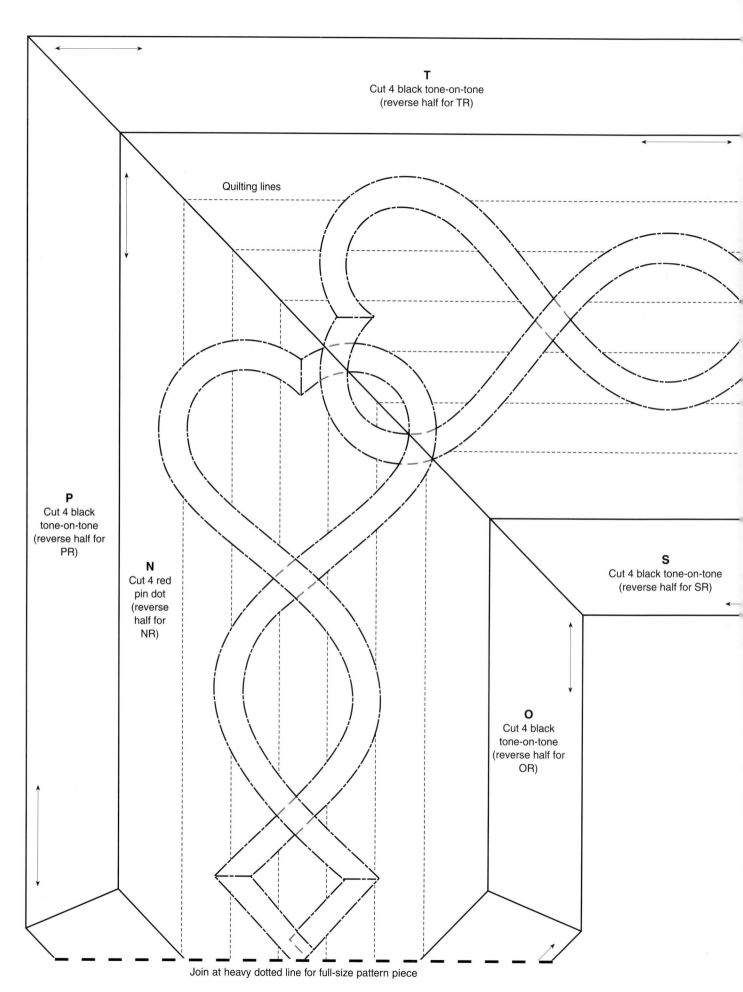

T
Cut 4 black tone-on-tone
(reverse half for TR)

Quilting lines

P
Cut 4 black
tone-on-tone
(reverse half for
PR)

N
Cut 4 red
pin dot
(reverse
half for
NR)

S
Cut 4 black tone-on-tone
(reverse half for SR)

O
Cut 4 black
tone-on-tone
(reverse half for
OR)

Join at heavy dotted line for full-size pattern piece

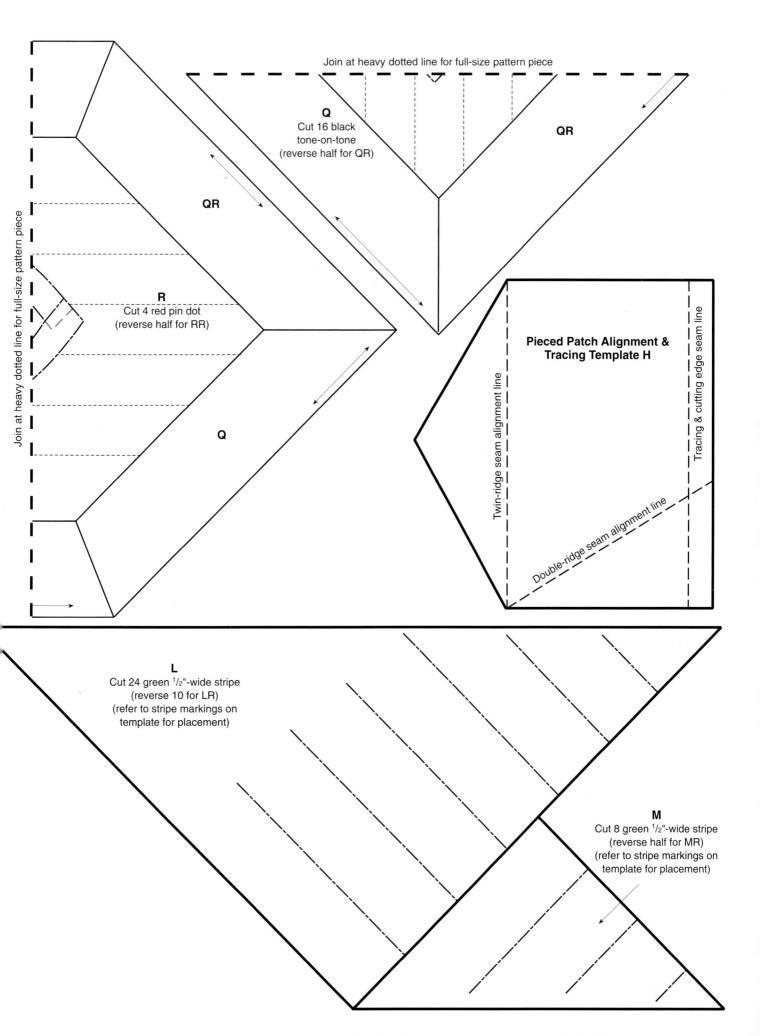

Join at heavy dotted line for full-size pattern piece

Q
Cut 16 black
tone-on-tone
(reverse half for QR)

QR

QR

Join at heavy dotted line for full-size pattern piece

R
Cut 4 red pin dot
(reverse half for RR)

Q

**Pieced Patch Alignment &
Tracing Template H**

Twin-ridge seam alignment line

Tracing & cutting edge seam line

Double-ridge seam alignment line

L
Cut 24 green ¹/₂"-wide stripe
(reverse 10 for LR)
(refer to stripe markings on
template for placement)

M
Cut 8 green ¹/₂"-wide stripe
(reverse half for MR)
(refer to stripe markings on
template for placement)

English Paper Piecing by Machine

Use your sewing machine with clear nylon monofilament and freezer paper to create perfect shapes while machine-zigzag stitching layers together.

1

PREPARATION

1A. Cut a section of freezer paper and fold in quarters. Place one foundation-diagram photocopy and staple through each diamond.

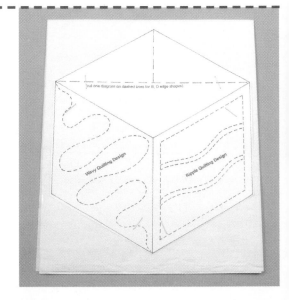

1B. Cut apart each stapled diamond stack. For edge shapes, some whole diamonds are divided further into halves and quarters; remove staples.

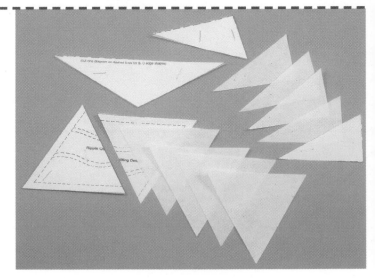

1C. Apply dabs of fabric glue stick to four points of paper side of each freezer-paper shape. Center on the backside of fabric patch.

1D. With tip and edge of medium-hot iron (cotton blend to wool range), fold seam allowance of one A diamond edge snugly around freezer-paper foundations to temporarily fuse and hold. Allow the tails to extend naturally.

2

SEWING

2A. Thread clear nylon monofilament or invisible thread through needle and bobbin. Adjust machine to multiple zigzag with narrow width and length. Align the center folded edges of two diamonds next to each other on the machine work surface so edges snugly touch with ends even. Tails at diamond tips should be overlapped by adjacent shape. If tails align in opposing directions, fold one back under its patch edge so that the diamond folded edges align properly. Zigzag-stitch across the two edges along the entire length while applying pressure to keep fabric folds closely aligned. A sample of white fabric and dark thread are shown in the photo since it is too difficult to see the monofilament thread on the dark fabric.

Tip
When slight differences in edge lengths occur, match ends, then ease/stretch to adjust edges as stitching progresses.

2B. Align and join third diamond folded edges in angle, allowing tails at tips to tuck under adjacent shape as before. Hold thread ends from previous seam to backside of work.

Tip
For optimum seam security (here with blocks and later with borders), take care to have stitches pierce points of all three shapes near corner intersections.

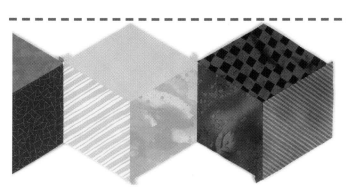

2C. Join cubes side by side in rows. Seam allowances of cubes at row ends remain flat, not iron-fused to the backside of diamonds.

2D. For panel top edge, join prepared quarter and long half diamonds along upper edge of cube row. Where seam allowances remain flat, align edge of paper foundation with adjacent shape point. Overlap flat seam allowance tails at panel edges.

2E. Join background row of prepared half and whole diamonds in angles of lower edge of cube row in the same fashion. Work in a continuous line of stitching, pivoting at angles, adding next shape in position without cutting threads.

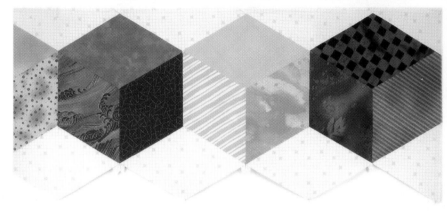

3 FINISHING

3A. When panel is complete, use rotary ruler to measure and cut excess seam allowance ¼" beyond exposed paper edge at panel underside.

3B. Remove paper by detaching glued areas and carefully pulling edges free from zigzag stitches.

Crayon Box Cubes

Try English paper piecing by machine to stitch this colorful crib quilt.

PROJECT SPECIFICATIONS
Skill Level: Beginner
Quilt Size: 45" x 57"

MATERIALS
- 4 different print scraps from 5 colors—turquoise, lime green, orange, yellow and violet
- ¼ yard contrasting print for narrow border
- 1 yard white-with-yellow dots for background
- 1⅜ yards yellow plaid for outer border and binding
- Thin cotton batting 51" x 63"
- Backing 51" x 63"
- Neutral color all-purpose thread
- Contrasting quilting threads
- Clear nylon monofilament
- Fabric glue stick
- 3½ yards 18"-wide plastic-coated freezer paper
- Stapler and staple remover
- Basic sewing tools and supplies, sewing machine with narrow width or variable multiple zigzag stitch, water-erasable marker or pencil, and template material

INSTRUCTIONS
Patch Preparation

Step 1. Prepare templates using pattern pieces given; cut as directed on each shape.

Step 2. Prepare six copies of Cube Paper-Foundation Diagram; cut out each whole cube shape, leaving a narrow margin around outside edges.

Tip
Foundation piecing of this project can be completed using conventional English paper piecing by hand. With that alternative, place freezer-paper shapes with plastic-coated side next to the wrong side of the fabric patches, then iron-fuse. Complete seam allowance folding and basting by hand; then join pieces by hand.

Step 3. Cut freezer paper into seven 17" lengths; fold each section into quarters. Place one copy of the foundation diagram on top of six sections. Staple through the stack at

both ends of each A diamond shape. Cut out each stapled A diamond stack exactly on outer solid lines. Remove staples as freezer-paper foundations are needed.

Step 4. Draw lines on remaining paper foundation copy to make B, C and D sections as shown in Figure 1.

Figure 1
Draw lines on foundation to
make B, C, D and DR sections.

Step 5. Staple through points as for A shapes; cut out shapes on printed and drawn lines to make B, C, D and DR foundation pieces as shown in Figure 2.

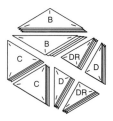

Figure 2
Cut out B, C, D and DR shapes.

Step 6. Apply glue stick to paper side of cut A shape at all four points. Center and secure each paper shape, placing paper side of foundation piece next to the wrong side of the fabric A piece. Prepare all A, B, C, D and DR pieces in the same fashion.

Step 7. Arrange three A diamonds from the same color group to form a cube shape as shown in Figure 3; repeat with all A shapes to form 20 cubes.

Figure 3
Position 3 A diamonds from the same
color group to form each hexagon cube.

Step 8. Arrange cubes to form five horizontal rows with four cubes in each row as shown in Figure 4.

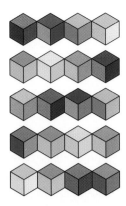

Figure 4
Arrange 4 cubes in 5 horizontal rows.

Step 9. Working on ironing-board surface, fold seam allowance of one fabric A diamond snugly around freezer-paper foundation and iron-fuse seam allowance to plastic coating. Repeat for remaining three edges of A. Place A back in cube shape; repeat with remaining two A shapes in the same cube. *Note: Do not fuse seam allowance of edges of A that are placed along the side edges of the center panel. These will remain flat, to be joined in regular seams later.* Allow excess seam allowance tails to extend naturally. Iron-fuse edges of all A diamonds.

Tip
Take care not to allow the hot iron to touch the freezer-paper's plastic coating. It can melt on contact and gum up the iron face plate and destroy the fusing capabilities of the freezer paper.

Step 10. Place B, C, D and DR in rows with cube shapes

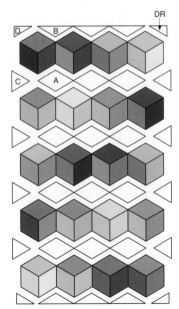

Figure 5
Arrange the background A diamonds between rows, C at row ends, B at top and bottom edges and D and DR at the corners.

and background A pieces as shown in Figure 5. Prepare B, C, D and DR pieces as for A, leaving one outer edge of B and C and two outer edges of D and DR unfused. *Note: These are joined in regular seams to border strips later.*

Joining Blocks for Center Panel

Step 1. Thread top of machine and bobbin with clear nylon monofilament. Test machine multiple zigzag set at a narrow width so that stitch side-to-side range is approximately $1/8$" to allow about $1/16$" of each patch edge to be secured by stitches while not interfering with paper removal later.

Tip
Investigate your machine's decorative stitch selection. Some stitch patterns other than the multiple zigzag can accomplish the joining and may add a designer touch at the same time.

Step 2. Assemble each cube by butting edges and zigzag stitching across vertical center seam of two lower A diamonds as shown in Figure 6. Tails should be allowed to tuck under adjacent folded edge of shape being joined. Position a third diamond in upper angle. Zigzag across edges, pivoting at center to complete seam in one operation.

Figure 6
Butt edges and zigzag-stitch across vertical center seam of 2 lower A diamonds.

Tip
Leave 1" or longer tails at each end of seam to secure. When adjacent shape is positioned to cross previous seam ends, tuck tails to backside of work.

Step 3. Zigzag vertical seams between units to join cubes in separate rows 1 through 5 as laid out.

Step 4. At top edge of panel, join D, DR and B to the upper edge of row 1. Position appropriate shape in the angle between cubes with edges abutted; zigzag to join. Begin stitching at raw edge of D or DR. As stitch/joining of one shape is completed, position next shape and continue stitching in one step across panel. Continue stitching to raw edge at row end.

Step 5. Join C and A to lower edge of row 1 in same manner. Continue joining cube rows 2 through 5 to previously assembled units, adding C and A shapes between rows.

When row 5 is in place, join D and DR and B pieces as in Step 4 to complete bottom edge of center panel; press.

Tip

Test iron heat to be sure it will not melt or damage clear nylon monofilament stitching prior to pressing actual patchwork. A too-hot iron will melt this type of thread.

Step 6. Place panel wrong side up on a rotary-cutting mat. Place 1/4" guideline of rotary ruler along exposed B, C and D paper edges; trim away any excess seam allowance beyond cutting edge to square-up panel. Remove paper foundations from all pieces.

Completing the Quilt Top

Step 1. Cut two 2" x 40½" E and two 2" x 28½" F strips white-with-yellow dots. Sew E to opposite long sides; press seams toward E.

Step 2. Cut one 2" x 2" square from four different print scraps for G. Sew G to each end of each F strip; sew an F-G strip to the top and bottom of the pieced center. Press seams toward F-G strips.

Step 3. Cut two 1½" x 43½" H and two 1½" x 33½" I strips contrasting print; sew H to opposite long sides and I to the top and bottom of the center panel; press seams toward strips.

Step 4. Cut four 6½" x 45½" J strips along the length of the yellow plaid. Sew a strip to opposite long sides and then to the top and bottom of the center panel; press seams toward strips.

Finishing the Quilt

Step 1. Transfer quilting lines to completed quilt top using patterns given for specific areas as marked on patterns.

Step 2. Sandwich thin cotton batting between the completed quilt top and prepared backing piece; pin or baste layers together to hold.

Step 3. Machine-quilt on marked lines or as desired using contrasting quilting threads. *Note: The sample was machine-quilted on marked lines and in the ditch of seams of pieces and borders.*

Crayon Box Cubes
Placement Diagram
45" x 57"

Tip

Machine quilting can be continuous within each cube. Begin at echo line near center, then stitch echo line and continue up and back on ripple lines in sequence when stitching reaches that portion of the design. When the circuit is complete, stitch across to corresponding starting point for next diamond and complete the circuit.

Step 4. When quilting is complete, remove pins or basting; trim batting and backing edges with quilted top. Transfer curved cutting line to corners; trim along curved corner cutting lines.

Step 5. Prepare 220" of 2¼"-wide bias binding from yellow plaid and apply to edges to finish. ❖

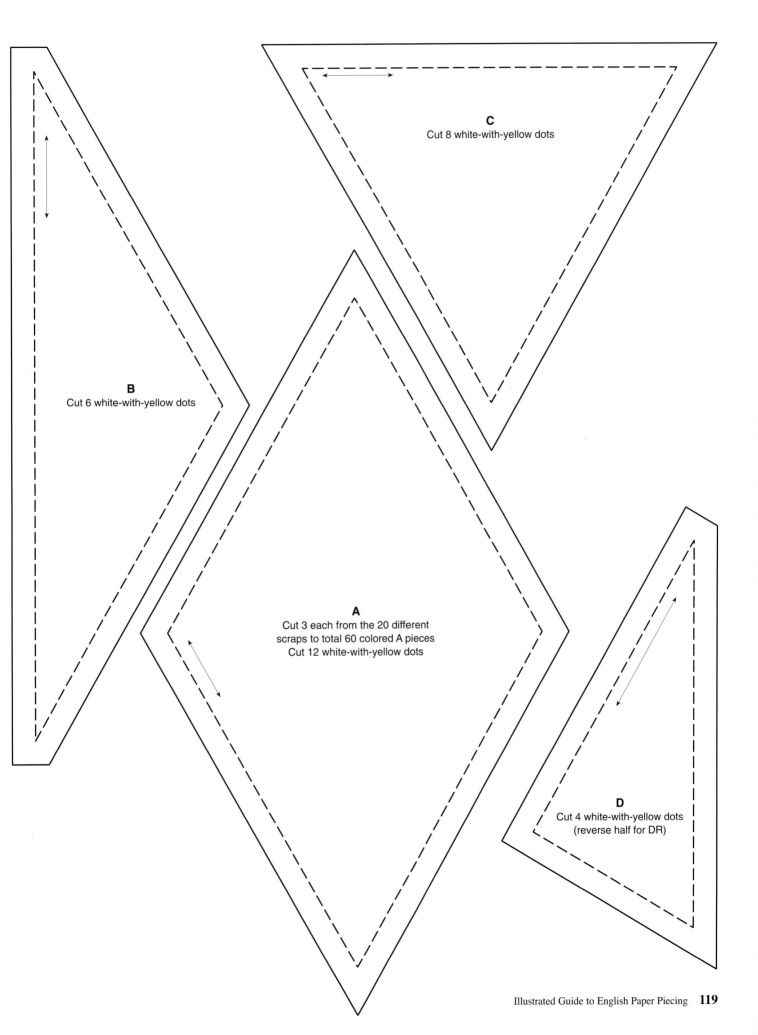

C
Cut 8 white-with-yellow dots

B
Cut 6 white-with-yellow dots

A
Cut 3 each from the 20 different
scraps to total 60 colored A pieces
Cut 12 white-with-yellow dots

D
Cut 4 white-with-yellow dots
(reverse half for DR)

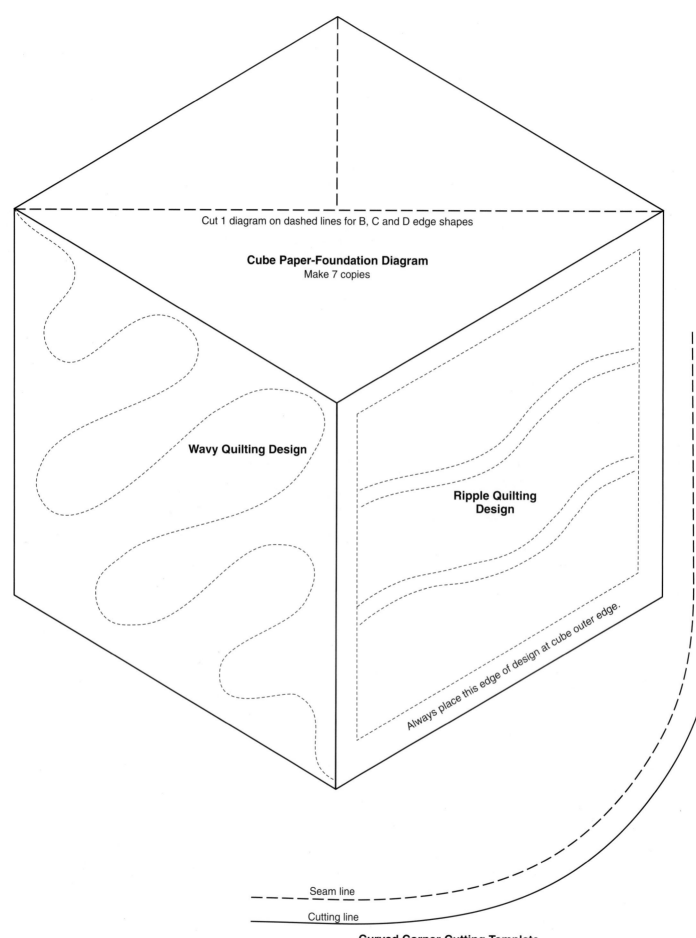

Cut 1 diagram on dashed lines for B, C and D edge shapes

Cube Paper-Foundation Diagram
Make 7 copies

Wavy Quilting Design

**Ripple Quilting
Design**

Always place this edge of design at cube outer edge.

Seam line

Cutting line

Curved Corner Cutting Template

120 *Master Quilter's Workshop*

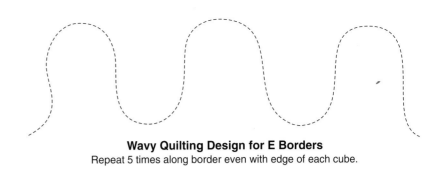

Wavy Quilting Design for E Borders
Repeat 5 times along border even with edge of each cube.

**Wavy
Quilting
Design for
Outer
Borders**
Repeat between
lines

**Wavy Quilting Design
for F Borders**
Repeat 4 times along border

Center width of design between 1/4" echo lines at border edges

English Paper Foundations for Diamonds

Diamond shapes may be accurately stitched using English paper foundations. The Entangled Lilies Piano Mat uses this simple technique.

1 PREPARING & CUTTING PIECES

1A. Use fabric glue stick to affix the paper foundation in place on the wrong side of the fabric. Fold seam allowance precisely over paper shape edge and baste, beginning at one narrow point end for every diamond of the project. Extend stitches deep into point to prepare accurate shape.

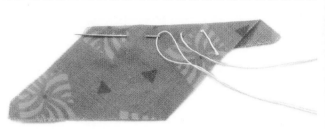

1B. As seam allowance is folded for subsequent edges, allow seam allowance tails to extend naturally away from the shape edge.

Back

Front

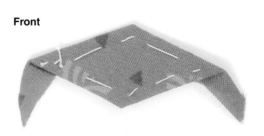

1C. Trim away some of the excess tails as the initial step in reducing bulk and interference.

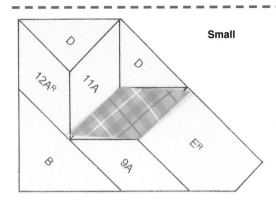

Small

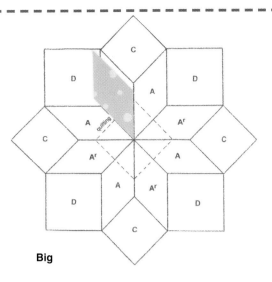

Big

1D. As piecing proceeds, take care to join appropriate edges. True diamonds will have four equal-length edges, any of which will match and fit together. Parallelogram designs will have pairs of long and short edges that will not all match and fit. Instead, shapes must be reversed to produce edges that will match. Diamond shapes in the Entangled Lilies Piano Mat and Aunt Seph's Recipe projects use parallelograms.

2

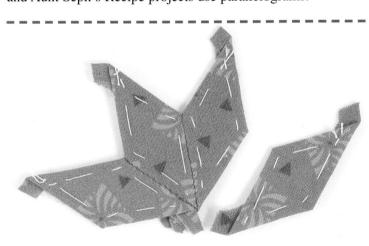

JOINING THE PIECES

2A. To prepare for joining, first position shapes in their intended layout. Rotate as necessary so that the tails at converging point ends are extended in the same direction. This will reduce interference from opposing tails in the finished seam.

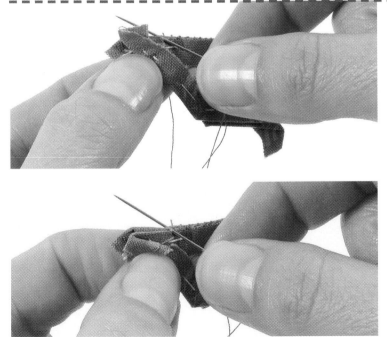

JOINING THE PIECES

2B. To join diamond patches, fold shapes right sides together with edges aligned. Stitch as usual, holding tails back and out of the way so that the folded edges are fully exposed even to points. Stitches pierce only the folded edges, not the tail extensions.

2C. To prepare the completed blossoms panel for joining to the center checker panel and surrounding borders on the Entangled Lilies Piano Mat, first press well. Then remove basting and paper foundations. Unfold and press outer-edge seam allowance flat. From the wrong side, position a straightedge exactly along the still-visible crease representing the seam line at the outer edge. Use a pencil or temporary marker to mark the seam line.

2D. Use a rotary cutter and ruler to trim excess seam allowance beyond the marked seam line. As pieced panel is aligned with center panels or borders for joining, align the newly trimmed edges with the raw edges. If seam allowance is too narrow to be trimmed, match marked seam line to the implied 1/4" seam line of the adjoining edge.

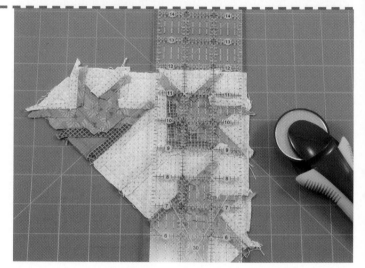

Entangled Lilies Piano Mat

Use English paper-foundation techniques to maintain accuracy when creating the pieced blossom sections of this pretty piano mat.

PROJECT SPECIFICATIONS

Skill Level: Intermediate

Mat Size: 38³/₄" x 10¹/₂"

MATERIALS

- Scraps taupe, dark salmon and light beige
- ¹/₈ yard each light taupe stripe and salmon
- ¹/₄ yard each cream with stars and dark brown print
- ¹/₃ yard beige dot
- Batting 41" x 13"
- Backing 41" x 13"
- Neutral color all-purpose thread
- Contrasting quilting thread
- Fabric glue stick
- Card stock
- Standard paper punch
- Basic sewing tools and supplies, water-erasable marker or pencil, and template material

INSTRUCTIONS

Making Blossom End Sections

Step 1. Make two photocopies of the Lilies Paper-Foundation Diagram.

Step 2. Cut apart paper foundation shapes A–F from copied sections.

Step 3. Using fabric glue stick, adhere each paper shape to the wrong side of the appropriate fabrics as marked on diagram, allowing space to add ¹/₄" seam allowance around each shape when cutting.

Step 4. Cut out shapes, adding a ¹/₄" seam allowance all around. Fold and baste seam allowances to the backside referring to English Paper Foundations for Diamonds on page 122.

Step 5. To assemble one side blossom unit, join two A and two AR pieces; set in one D, one DD and one E and add B referring to Figure 1; repeat for two side blossom units and two reversed units.

Step 6. To assemble one end

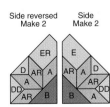

Figure 1
Join pieces as shown to make side blossom units.

blossom unit, join two A and two AR pieces; set in C and DD and add B referring to Figure 2; repeat for two units.

Figure 2
Join pieces as shown to make end blossom unit.

Step 7. Join one end blossom unit, a side blossom unit and a side blossom reversed unit with F and FR to complete one blossom end section as shown in Figure 3; press. Repeat for two blossom end sections.

Figure 3
Join 1 end blossom unit, a side blossom unit and a side blossom reversed unit with F and FR to complete 1 blossom end section.

Step 8. Remove all foundation papers; unfold and finger-press seam allowance at outer edge flat. Use a straightedge and pencil to mark the position of panel outer crease all around on the wrong side of each end section. Trim excess seam allowance to beyond creased lines ¹/₄".

Step 9. Cut two 3⁵/₈" x 8¹/₄" G pieces from beige dot. Sew G to each blossom end section as shown in Figure 4; press seams toward G.

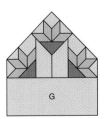

Figure 4
Sew G to each blossom end section.

Step 10. Transfer solid line only of stem position to each end section using the water-erasable marker or pencil.

Step 11. Prepare six 8" lengths of ¼" finished width dark brown print bias strips (see Step 6 of Appliqué Details of Twelve Days of Christmas on page 93).

Step 12. Position each length along marked guidelines; baste to hold. *Note: Gray lines on pattern indicate sections of stems that are placed under other stem sections.*

Step 13. Release one or two stitches of the end blossom unit B seam and insert stem under B edges as shown in Figure 5. Release stitches at bottom edge of the side blossom unit B seams and insert stems under B edges; fold excess back toward G, again referring to Figure 5.

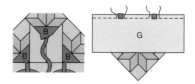

Figure 5
Release 1 or 2 stitches of the B seam
and insert stems under B edges.

Step 14. Complete appliqué stitching of all stem edges, trimming and rounding ends to match diagram.

Step 15. Referring to Steps 5–7 for Gifts From an English Garden on page 81, prepare and attach six dark salmon punch dots at indicated positions opposite the stem ends

eferring to the Lilies Paper-Foundation Paper Diagram or placement.

Making Checker Center Panel

Step 1. Cut five $1\frac{1}{2}$" x 14" strips each light beige and taupe scraps.

Step 2. Join two light beige strips with three taupe strips with right sides together along length to make an H strip set; press seams toward darker fabric. Repeat with two taupe strips and three light beige strips to make an I strip set; press seams toward darker fabric.

Step 3. Cut the H strip set into nine $1\frac{1}{2}$" segments and the I strip set into eight $1\frac{1}{2}$" segments as shown in Figure 6.

Figure 6
Cut strip sets into
$1\frac{1}{2}$" segments for H
and I as shown.

Step 4. Join H and I segments to complete checker center panel as shown in Figure 7; press seams toward H.

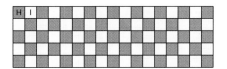

Figure 7
Join H and I segments to
complete checker center panel.

Adding Borders

Step 1. Cut two $\frac{7}{8}$" x $17\frac{1}{2}$" J and two $\frac{7}{8}$" x $6\frac{1}{4}$" K strips light taupe stripe with stripe running across the narrow width of the strips. Sew J to opposite long sides and K to narrow ends of the pieced center section; press seams toward strips.

Step 2. Cut two $1\frac{1}{2}$" x $18\frac{1}{4}$" L strips beige dot; sew a strip to opposite long sides of the pieced center section. Press seams toward L.

Step 3. Sew an end section to each short end of the pieced center section; press seams toward end sections.

Step 4. Cut two $7/8$" x 29" M, two $7/8$" x 7" N and two $7/8$" x $7^{1}/2$" O strips light taupe stripe as in Step 1. Center and sew M to opposite long sides of the pieced center section, extending ends as shown in Figure 8; press seams toward strips.

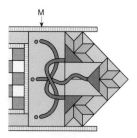

Figure 8
Center and sew M to opposite long
sides of the pieced center section,
extending ends as shown.

Step 5. Using a straightedge and rotary cutter, trim ends of M even with the angle of the end sections as shown in Figure 9.

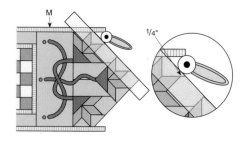

Figure 9
Using a straight edge and rotary cutter, trim ends
of M even with the angle of the end sections.

Step 6. Add N and O strips, pressing and trimming as in Steps 4 and 5.

Step 7. Cut two $1^{1}/2$" x 29" P, two $1^{1}/2$" x 9" Q and two $1^{1}/2$" x 11" R strips cream with stars. Sew P to opposite long sides and Q and R to ends as in Steps 4 and 5 to complete the pieced top.

Finishing the Mat

Step 1. Crease and press under the raw edges of the quilt top $1/4$" all around; unfold. ***Note****: To ensure accurate outer border width while creasing the folded edge, measure the finished border width with a gridded ruler from the wrong side; score the seam line with a tracing wheel or a semisharp plastic edge.*

Step 2. Sandwich thin cotton batting between backing and completed top; pin or baste to hold.

Step 3. Quilt in the ditch around center patchwork, between borders, in pieced blossom sections and around appliqué shapes using contrasting quilting thread.

Step 4. When quilting is complete, remove pins or basting. Trim batting and backing edges even with edges of the quilted top; then trim batting $3/8$" smaller all around.

Step 5. Refold edge of pieced top; mark and crease backing at edge seam line (exactly matching folded edge of top). Fold seam allowance under.

Step 6. Bring folded edges of quilt top and backing together, pin and topstitch by hand or machine to finish. ❖

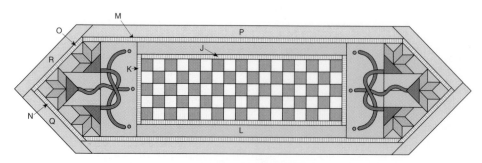

Entangled Lilies Piano Mat
Placement Diagram
$38^{3}/4$" x $10^{1}/2$"

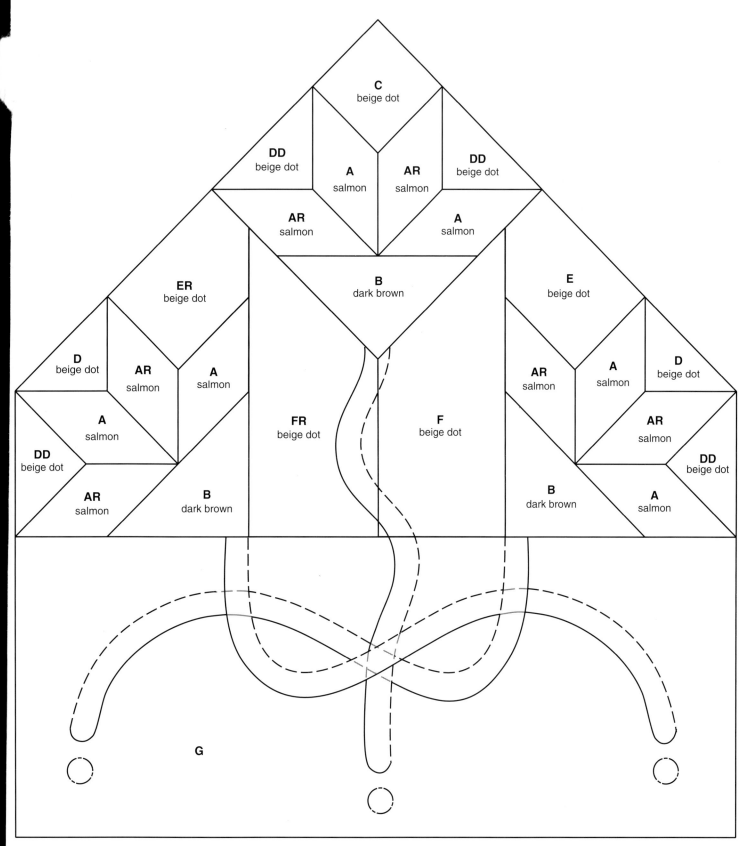

Lilies Paper-Foundation Diagram
Make 2 photocopies

Metric Conversion Charts

Metric Conversions

U.S. Measurement		Multiplied by		Metric Measurement
yards	x	.9144	=	meters (m)
yards	x	91.44	=	centimeters (cm)
inches	x	2.54	=	centimeters (cm)
inches	x	25.40	=	millimeters (mm)
inches	x	.0254	=	meters (m)

Metric Measurement		Multiplied by		U.S. Measurement
centimeters	x	.3937	=	inches
meters	x	1.0936	=	yards

Standard Equivalents

U.S. Measurement		Metric Measurement		
1/8 inch	=	3.20 mm	=	0.32 cm
1/4 inch	=	6.35 mm	=	0.635 cm
3/8 inch	=	9.50 mm	=	0.95 cm
1/2 inch	=	12.70 mm	=	1.27 cm
5/8 inch	=	15.90 mm	=	1.59 cm
3/4 inch	=	19.10 mm	=	1.91 cm
7/8 inch	=	22.20 mm	=	2.22 cm
1 inch	=	25.40 mm	=	2.54 cm
1/8 yard	=	11.43 cm	=	0.11 m
1/4 yard	=	22.86 cm	=	0.23 m
3/8 yard	=	34.29 cm	=	0.34 m
1/2 yard	=	45.72 cm	=	0.46 m
5/8 yard	=	57.15 cm	=	0.57 m
3/4 yard	=	68.58 cm	=	0.69 m
7/8 yard	=	80.00 cm	=	0.80 m
1 yard	=	91.44 cm	=	0.91 m

U.S. Measurement		Metric Measurement		
1 1/8 yard	=	102.87 cm	=	1.03 m
1 1/4 yard	=	114.30 cm	=	1.14 m
1 3/8 yard	=	125.73 cm	=	1.26 m
1 1/2 yard	=	137.16 cm	=	1.37 m
1 5/8 yard	=	148.59 cm	=	1.49 m
1 3/4 yard	=	160.02 cm	=	1.60 m
1 7/8 yard	=	171.44 cm	=	1.71 m
2 yards	=	182.88 cm	=	1.83 m
2 1/8 yards	=	194.31 cm	=	1.94 m
2 1/4 yards	=	205.74 cm	=	2.06 m
2 3/8 yards	=	217.17 cm	=	2.17 m
2 1/2 yards	=	228.60 cm	=	2.29 m
2 5/8 yards	=	240.03 cm	=	2.40 m
2 3/4 yards	=	251.46 cm	=	2.51 m
2 7/8 yards	=	262.88 cm	=	2.63 m
3 yards	=	274.32 cm	=	2.74 m
3 1/8 yards	=	285.75 cm	=	2.86 m
3 1/4 yards	=	297.18 cm	=	2.97 m
3 3/8 yards	=	308.61 cm	=	3.09 m
3 1/2 yards	=	320.04 cm	=	3.20 m
3 5/8 yards	=	331.47 cm	=	3.31 m
3 3/4 yards	=	342.90 cm	=	3.43 m
3 7/8 yards	=	354.32 cm	=	3.54 m
4 yards	=	365.76 cm	=	3.66 m
4 1/8 yards	=	377.19 cm	=	3.77 m
4 1/4 yards	=	388.62 cm	=	3.89 m
4 3/8 yards	=	400.05 cm	=	4.00 m
4 1/2 yards	=	411.48 cm	=	4.11 m
4 5/8 yards	=	422.91 cm	=	4.23 m
4 3/4 yards	=	434.34 cm	=	4.34 m
4 7/8 yards	=	445.76 cm	=	4.46 m
5 yards	=	457.20 cm	=	4.57 m